SAINT JOSEPH

PRAYER BOOK

SAINT JOSEPH

PRAYER BOOK

Written, compiled, and edited
by Mary Mark Wickenhiser, FSP

Pauline
BOOKS & MEDIA
Boston

Nihil Obstat: Reverend Thomas K. Macdonald, S.T.D.

Imprimatur: ✠ Seán Cardinal O'Malley, O.F.M. Cap.
Archbishop of Boston
February 26, 2021

ISBN 10: 0-8198-9150-9

ISBN 13: 978-0-8198-9150-1

Art and cover design by Ryan MacQuade

Published by Pauline Books & Media, 50 Saint Pauls Avenue, Boston, MA 02130-3491

Printed in the U.S.A.

www.pauline.org

Pauline Books & Media is the publishing house of the Daughters of St. Paul, an international congregation of women religious serving the Church with the communications media.

1 2 3 4 5 6 7 8 9   25 24 23 22 21

There are many saints to whom God has given the power to assist us in the necessities of life, but the power given to Saint Joseph is unlimited: it extends to all our needs, and all those who invoke him with confidence are sure to be heard.

SAINT THOMAS AQUINAS

Contents

SAINT JOSEPH
MODEL OF THE INTERIOR LIFE

SAINT JOSEPH

Strength of Fathers and Pillar of Family Life

SAINT JOSEPH

Model of Workers and Patron of Divine Providence

SAINT JOSEPH

Terror of Demons

SAINT JOSEPH
Guardian of Purity

SAINT JOSEPH
Patron of a Happy Death

SAINT JOSEPH
PROTECTOR OF THE UNIVERSAL CHURCH

SAINT JOSEPH
PRAYERS, DEVOTIONS, AND PRACTICES TO HONOR HIM

Prayers

Devotions

Practices

Acknowledgments

EVERY EFFORT HAS been made to trace copyright holders and to obtain their permission for the use of copyright material. The publisher apologizes for any errors or omissions in the above list and would be grateful if notified of any corrections that should be incorporated in future reprints or editions of this book.

Temptation by Father Cassidy Stinson, used with permission.

Holy Cloak of Saint Joseph is based on the version by the Pious Union of Saint Joseph (pusj.org).

The Novena for Families adapted from an earlier version published in 2000 by Pauline Books & Media.

The Novena to Find Employment adapted from an earlier version published in 2000 by Pauline Books & Media.

All other prayers are adapted from common sources, unless otherwise indicated.

General Introduction

THE STORY OF Saint Joseph paints a picture of an ordinary man, living what appeared to be an ordinary life, but fulfilling an extraordinary mission entrusted to him by God. Although no words of Saint Joseph are recorded in the Gospels, his silent example of fidelity, integrity, protection, duty, and care for the Holy Family tells us quite a bit about him and makes him one of the most beloved saints of the Christian world. While details of his life may be lacking—disregarding the apocryphal sources of unreliable narratives from the early centuries—we can still gather credible facts about him from Scripture, history scholars, Church Fathers and Mothers, and Ecclesial writings. He was born of a royal and princely line, a descendant of King David (Mt 1:1–16); he was the lawful husband of Mary, the Virgin Mother of Jesus Christ, and therefore he was the legally recognized father or "foster father" of the

Redeemer of the world (Mt 1:24–25); he was a "just man" who deeply loved his wife and the child born of her (Mt 1:19); he suffered hardship to protect them from danger (Mt 2:13–16) and worked long hours at his carpentry trade (Mt 13:55) to provide for their needs (Lk 2:24). After the incident of the losing and finding of Jesus in the Temple when he was twelve, there is no further mention of Joseph. But as is often the case in Scripture, a few simple statements can provide material for worthy reflection.

"[Mary] was found to be with child . . ." (Mt 1:18). What Joseph understood about the situation and what his motives were in deciding to quietly divorce Mary are not entirely clear. Since the angel later tells Joseph that "the child who has been conceived in her is from the Holy Spirit" (Mt 1:20) it would seem that he had not known this and was acting under the assumption that she had been unfaithful.

But some early Church Fathers held that Mary must have told Joseph what happened and that he made his decision out of a sense of reverence, feeling unworthy to be part of God's plan that was coming to pass in Mary. In either case, after a dream in which he is given an explanation (Mt 1:20–25), "Joseph obeyed the explicit command of the angel and took Mary into his house, while respecting the fact that she belonged exclusively to God" (*Guardian of the Redeemer*, 20).

Historians tell us that Jewish men generally married between the ages of sixteen and twenty-four. In all probability, then, Saint Joseph married when he was in his late teens or early twenties. To fill the role of guardian, provider, and protector, it seems that God would choose a vibrant young man rather than a pious older man with white hair, which was a popular depiction in the Middle Ages based on fictional narratives attempting to safeguard the universal belief in Mary's virginity.

Joseph "did as the angel of the Lord had commanded him and took his wife into his house" (Mt 1:24). By accepting an event that transcended human understanding, Joseph welcomed into his house not only Mary and the child growing in her womb, but he also welcomed the work of the Holy Spirit that would affect the rest of his life. As the events of their life together unfolded—the journey to Bethlehem, the birth of the child, the visit of the Magi, the flight into Egypt, their return and settling in Nazareth, the losing and finding of Jesus in the Temple, the journey back to their home and the hidden years—Joseph was cooperating in the mystery of salvation, entrusted with the task of *raising* Jesus. Feeding, clothing, educating Jesus in the Law, and teaching him a trade as the duties of a father required.

"Then [Jesus] went down with them and went to Nazareth, and he was subject to them" (Lk 2:51).

The *hidden years* of the Holy Family are even more latent in regard to Saint Joseph. The Gospels speak no more of him other than when the town's folk referred to Jesus as "the carpenter's son" (Mt 13:55). The events of those *hidden years* and the circumstances of the death of Saint Joseph are left to our reflection. What we can be sure of is that Joseph continued to be the faithful servant of the Lord, serving him in those he was given to care for, and he remained the faithful cooperator in God's great design for the salvation of mankind. In his homily on the feast of Saint Joseph (March 2014), Pope Francis offers us some insights for reflection on those hidden years: "Joseph also quietly imparted to Jesus that wisdom which consists above all in reverence for the Lord, prayer and fidelity to his word, and obedience to his will. Joseph's paternal example helped Jesus to grow, on a human level, in his understanding and appreciation of his unique relationship to his heavenly Father."

Devotion to Saint Joseph

From the earliest times in the life of the Church Saint Joseph was accepted as head of the Holy Family, and his life was woven into the mysteries of Christ's infancy and childhood; tribute granted to Joseph was always in connection with the veneration of Mary and the adoration of Jesus. In the third century we find the first authentic sculpture of Joseph on a marble plaque in the cemetery of Priscilla—a rough drawing of the Magi scene with the child Jesus sitting on Mary's lap and Saint Joseph directly behind her, pointing to the star. Other images of Joseph appear in the six mosaics on the triumphal arch of the Church of Saint Mary Major at Rome, built in 435 by Pope Sixtus III to commemorate the Council of Ephesus, which defined the dogma of Mary as the Mother of God.

During the reign of Roman Emperor Constantine (fourth century) Saint Helena had a church built in

Nazareth in honor of Saint Joseph. By the seventh century there is information that in the town of Nazareth two large churches had been built—one commemorating the location of the Annunciation and the other honoring the house where Mary and Joseph lived. Although there is no indication of a special devotion to Joseph, there is reason to believe that he was held in high esteem and venerated because of his relationship with Jesus and Mary. In seventh-century Egypt, a feast was instituted to commemorate the death of Saint Joseph.

During the early medieval period, sometimes referred to as the Dark Ages, the writings of prominent abbots indicate a growing devotion to Mary, Mother of God, and an increase in esteem for Saint Joseph. Veneration for Saint Joseph found its beginnings in monasteries and devotion to him grew through the centuries. In the later Middle Ages Saints Albert the Great, Thomas Aquinas, Bernard of Clairvaux, Bernardine of Siena, and others wrote treatises and delivered sermons on the virtues and merits of Saint Joseph. Later writings on Saint Joseph all drew from the rich theological reflections of this period. One of the first scholarly works on the life, death, and heavenly glory of Saint Joseph, entitled *Summary of the Gifts of Saint Joseph*, was written by the Dominican Isidoro Isolano.

The Council of Trent (1545–1563) extended the feast of Saint Joseph (March 19) to the whole Catholic world, and new foundations of religious orders placed themselves under the patronage of Saint Joseph.

In 1870, during a time of political upheaval for the Vatican, Pope Pius IX placed the entire Church under the protection of Saint Joseph, naming him as Patron of the Universal Church; the following year he declared March 19 as the official feast of Saint Joseph.

The encyclical letter of Leo XIII, *Quamquam Pluries* issued in 1889, was the first to outline a theology of Saint Joseph and urged all Catholics to pray to him as Patron of the Universal Church: "The special motives for which Saint Joseph has been proclaimed Patron of the Church, and from which the Church looks for singular benefit from his patronage and protection, are that Joseph was the spouse of Mary and that he was reputed the father of Jesus Christ. From these sources have sprung his dignity, his holiness, his glory" (*Quamquam Pluries*, 3).

As a response to the May Day celebration for workers supported by Communist-held countries, Pope Pius XII introduced the feast of Saint Joseph the Worker. By the work of his hands and the sweat of his brow, Joseph provided for the needs of Jesus and Mary. All working people should look to Joseph as their father and defender, obtaining protection and assistance in their time of need.

In 1989 Saint John Paul II issued the apostolic exhortation *Redemptoris Custos* (*Guardian of the Redeemer*) on the person and mission of Saint Joseph in the life of Christ and of the Church. The occasion was the one hundredth anniversary of *Quamquam Pluries,* and John Paul briefly reflects on the Gospel texts that refer to Saint Joseph. He remarks on how the time of the hidden years of Jesus was entrusted to Joseph's guardianship, and that in the love of Joseph, Mary, and Jesus, families today can find a model of encouragement and strength to share their lives together in an environment of love. John Paul not only urges the faithful to turn to Saint Joseph with great confidence, but also to reflect on and imitate his humble, mature manner of service to others, thus cooperating in God's plan of salvation.

In 2020, Pope Francis issued an apostolic letter, *Patris Corde* (*With a Father's Heart*), on the 150th anniversary of the declaration of Saint Joseph as Patron of the Universal Church. He reflected on Saint Joseph as a tender and loving father, and encouraged the faithful to follow the example of Joseph's obedience, acceptance, and courage.

Whether you have a long-standing relationship with Saint Joseph or you are just setting out on your path of devotion to him, it is with confidence in Saint Joseph's desire to be provider, protector, and patron to everyone who calls on him that the prayers and reflections herein are offered. May the words of Saint Teresa of Ávila be of encouragement to you: "I do not remember even now that I have ever asked anything of Saint Joseph which he has failed to grant. . . . To other saints the Lord seems to have given power to help us in some special necessity, but to this glorious saint, I know by experience, he has given the power to help us in them all" (*Autobiography*, VI, 9).

EVERYDAY
PRAYERS

The Sign of the Cross

English:

In the name of the Father, and of the Son, and of the Holy Spirit. Amen.

Latin:

In nomine Patris, et Filii, et Spiritus Sancti. Amen.

The Lord's Prayer

English:

Our Father, who art in heaven, hallowed be thy name; thy kingdom come; thy will be done on earth as it is in heaven. Give us this day our daily bread, and forgive us our trespasses, as we forgive those who trespass against us, and lead us not into temptation, but deliver us from evil. Amen.

Latin:

Pater Noster, qui es in caelis, sanctificetur nomen tuum. Adveniat regnum tuum. Fiat voluntas tua, sicut in caelo et in terra. Panem nostrum quotidianum da nobis hodie, et dimitte nobis debita nostra sicut et nos dimittimus debitoribus nostris. Et ne nos inducas in tentationem, sed libera nos a malo. Amen.

Hail Mary

English:

Hail Mary, full of grace, the Lord is with thee. Blessed art thou among women, and blessed is the fruit of thy womb, Jesus. Holy Mary, Mother of God, pray for us sinners, now and at the hour of our death. Amen.

Latin:

Ave Maria, gratia plena, Dominus tecum. Benedicta tu in mulieribus, et benedictus fructus ventris tui, Iesus. Sancta Maria, Mater Dei, ora pro nobis peccatoribus, nunc, et in hora mortis nostrae. Amen.

Glory

English:

Glory to the Father, and to the Son, and to the Holy Spirit, as it was in the beginning, is now, and will be forever. Amen.

Latin:

Gloria Patri, et Filio, et Spiritui Sancto. Sicut erat in principio, et nunc, et semper, et in saecula saeculorum. Amen.

The Morning Offering

O Jesus, through the Immaculate Heart of Mary, I offer you all my prayers, works, joys, and sufferings of this day, for the intentions of your Sacred Heart, in union with the holy Sacrifice of the Mass throughout the world, in reparation for my sins, for the intentions of my loved ones, and for the general intention recommended this month by the Holy Father.

Offering of Oneself to the Holy Spirit

Divine Holy Spirit,
love of the Father and of the Son,
through the hands of Mary, your most pure spouse,
and upon the altar of the heart of Jesus,
I offer you myself today
and every day of my life.
I offer you my daily labors;
my every action, my every breath,
with all my love and every beat of my heart.
Grant that today and every day I may
heed your inspiration and, in all things,
accomplish your will. Amen.

Adoration and Praise

I adore you, my God, and I love you with all my heart. I thank you for having created me, made me a Christian, and sustained me through the night. I offer you my actions of this day: grant that they all may be according to your will and for your greater glory. Preserve me from sin and all evil today. May your grace be always with me and with all whom I love. Amen.

The Angelus

℣. The Angel of the Lord declared unto Mary,

℟. And she conceived of the Holy Spirit.

Hail Mary . . .

℣. Behold the handmaid of the Lord,

℟. Be it done unto me according to thy word.

Hail Mary . . .

℣. And the Word was made flesh,

℟. And dwelt among us.

Hail Mary . . .

℣. Pray for us, O holy Mother of God,

℟. That we may be made worthy of the promises of Christ.

Let us pray.

Pour forth, we beseech thee, O Lord, thy grace into our hearts: that we, to whom the Incarnation of Christ, thy Son, was made known by the message of an Angel, may by his Passion and Cross be brought to the glory of his Resurrection. Through the same Christ our Lord. Amen.

Glory be . . .

The Regina Caeli

(Prayed during the Easter season instead of the Angelus.)

℣. Queen of heaven, rejoice, alleluia:

℟. For he whom you merited to bear, alleluia,

℣. Has risen, as he said, alleluia.

℟. Pray for us to God, alleluia.

℣. Rejoice and be glad, O Virgin Mary, alleluia.

℟. For the Lord has truly risen, alleluia.

Let us pray.

O God, you mercifully brought joy into the world by the resurrection of your Son, Our Lord Jesus Christ. Grant that we may come to the joy of everlasting life through the prayers of his mother, the Virgin Mary. Through the same Christ our Lord. Amen.

Glory be . . .

An Act of Faith

O my God, I firmly believe that you are one God in three divine Persons: Father, Son, and Holy Spirit; I believe that your divine Son became man and died for our sins, and that he will come to judge the living and the dead. I believe these and all the truths which the holy Catholic Church teaches, because you have revealed them, who can neither deceive nor be deceived.

An Act of Hope

O my God, relying on your infinite goodness and promises, I hope to obtain pardon of my sins, the help of your grace, and life everlasting, through the merits of Jesus Christ, my Lord and Redeemer.

An Act of Love

O my God, I love you above all things, with my whole heart and soul, because you are all-good and worthy of all love. I love my neighbor as myself for the love of you. I forgive all who have injured me, and I ask pardon of all whom I have injured.

An Act of Contrition

O my God, I am heartily sorry for having offended you, and I detest all my sins, because of your just punishments, but most of all because they offend you, my God, who are all-good and deserving of all my love. I firmly resolve, with the help of your grace, to sin no more and to avoid the near occasions of sin.

Prayer of Entrustment

Dear and loving Mother Mary, keep your hand upon me this day; guard my mind, my heart, and my senses, that I may not commit sin. Make my thoughts, affections, words, and actions holy, so that I may be pleasing to you and to your divine Son, Jesus, and attain heaven with you.

Jesus and Mary, give me your holy blessing: In the name of the Father, and of the Son, and of the Holy Spirit. Amen.

Hail, Holy Queen

Hail, Holy Queen, Mother of Mercy, our life, our sweetness, and our hope! To thee we cry, poor banished children of Eve. To thee we send up our sighs, mourning and weeping in this valley of tears. Turn then, most gracious advocate, thine eyes of mercy toward us, and after this our exile, show unto us the blessed fruit of thy womb, Jesus. O clement, O loving, O sweet Virgin Mary.

The Memorare

Remember, O most gracious Virgin Mary, that never was it know that anyone who fled to thy protection, implored thy help, or sought thy intercession was left unaided. Inspired with this confidence, I fly unto thee, O Virgin of virgins, my Mother. To thee do I come, before thee I stand, sinful and sorrowful. O Mother of the Word Incarnate, despise not my petitions, but in thy mercy hear and answer me. Amen.

To the Guardian Angel

Angel of God, my guardian dear, to whom God's love entrusts me here, ever this day/night be at my side, to light and guard, to rule and guide. Amen.

For the Faithful Departed

Eternal rest grant unto them, O Lord,
and let perpetual light shine upon them.
May they rest in peace. Amen.

SAINT JOSEPH

MODEL OF THE INTERIOR LIFE

The Gospels speak exclusively of what Joseph "did." Still, they allow us to discover in his "actions"—shrouded in silence as they are—an aura of deep contemplation. Joseph was in daily contact with the mystery "hidden from ages past," and which "dwelt" under his roof.

Saint John Paul II,
Guardian of the Redeemer, 25

Introduction

THE INTERIOR LIFE, as spoken of by saints and sages, refers to our relationship with God, the union of friendship that grows through regular and candid conversation with Christ. And how can I give attention to this interior life when my time and energy need to be focused on my "exterior life"—on many other concerns that impact my life and those of my loved ones?

Unlike us, Saint Joseph had little problem engaging God in conversation; he had Jesus and the Blessed Mother with him all the time and spent a great part of his life in close companionship with them. But his life was not all ecstasies and raptures. Like us he had concerns, problems, and challenges. He had to work hard to provide for his family; while in a foreign land he had to keep Jesus and Mary safe; he had to protect them when they traveled; when they arrived in Nazareth, it was Joseph's responsibility to secure housing for his family and establish himself in his trade as a carpenter.

What was his secret to a deeper interior life? Saint Joseph turned his everyday life and work into prayer, and he can teach us to do the same. He can teach us how to listen to God in prayer, to acknowledge God's will in the everyday circumstances of life, and to embrace that will faithfully when it is made known. It was through prayer that Saint Joseph found his strength and courage; he did not expect God to adapt to his wishes, but rather he adapted to the circumstances, did what he could and should, and then relied on God for the rest. Trust Saint Joseph to show you how to turn your ordinary actions into a life of continual prayer.

Morning Prayer

MORNING PRAYER IS a time to praise and thank God for all the blessings we have received from his goodness and love. Lifting our heart and mind to God in the early hours of the day can help us put our life into perspective and focus on the things that are truly important. God, our Father and Creator, welcomes our prayer and watches over us with compassion and mercy.

While praying the psalms, keep in mind that Saint Joseph, himself, would have chanted or recited verses of the psalms from memory as part of his own morning ritual of prayer.

> I will bless the Lord at all times,
> His praise will be ever on my lips.
> Glory be to the Father, and to the Son, and to
>   the Holy Spirit,
> As it was in the beginning, is now, and will be
>   forever. Amen.

You may choose other Psalms of praise and thanksgiving from your Bible.

Psalm 92

It is good to praise and thank the Lord.

It is good to give thanks to the LORD,
    to sing psalms to your name, Most High;
to declare your loving kindness in the morning
    and your faithfulness every night,
with the sound of a ten-stringed lyre,
    and the music of a harp.
For you, LORD, have made me rejoice because of
        your works,
    I shout for joy at the works of your hands.
How great, O LORD, are your deeds,
how deep your designs.

Glory be . . .

Psalm 112

The Lord blesses those who love him.

Happy are those who fear the LORD,
    who joyfully keep his commandments.
Their children will be powerful in the land;
    the descendants of the upright shall be blessed.
    Their righteous conduct shall stand forever.
Merciful, compassionate, and righteous,

in the darkness they rise like a light for the
upright.
The righteous will be held in everlasting
remembrance.
They will never be afraid of bad reports,
Their hearts are steadfast for they trust in the
LORD.
Lavishly they sow and give to the poor;
their righteousness endures forever.

Glory be . . .

The Word of God
Matthew 6:19–21

The following Gospel passage could well describe Saint Joseph's plan of life—to see God's will in the circumstances of life, meeting the challenges and storing them up as treasures for heaven. Living moment by moment, as best we can, in God's presence, gives genuine purpose to our lives. When we put God in first place, the things of this earth become stepping-stones to God.

"Do not store up treasures for yourselves on earth, where moth and rust destroy, and where thieves break in and steal; Store up treasures for yourselves in heaven, where neither moth nor rust destroy, and where thieves neither break in nor steal. For where your treasure is, there will your heart be too."

Open my heart, Lord, to the power of your word.

From prayer we draw the strength we need to meet the challenges of daily life as committed followers of Jesus Christ; as such we can become living signs of the Lord's loving presence to those around us.

Heavenly Father, I thank you for the gift of a new day and come before you to seek your graces and blessing:

Open the eyes of my heart that I may recognize your loving Providence at work in the events of this day.

Response: *Lord, keep me mindful of your love today.*

Inspire my thoughts, works, and actions that I may be a source of joy and consolation for all those I meet today. ℟.

Be with me today so that in all I say and do, I may be a living witness of your love and mercy. ℟.

Grant that all those I love may be kept from harm this day. Ŗ.

(Add you own general and particular intentions.)

Conclude your intercessions by praying to our heavenly Father in the words Jesus taught us:

Our Father, p. 13.

Closing Prayer

Father in heaven, hear my morning prayer; let the splendor of your love light my way that I may spend this day in joy of spirit and peace of mind. Grant this through Jesus Christ, your Son. Amen.

After the closing prayer you may want to add one of the following prayers to Saint Joseph.

To Saint Joseph, the Worker, p. 76, or For One's Family, p. 49.

Let us praise the Lord.
And give him thanks.

Evening Prayer

AS THE DAY draws to a close, we quiet our mind and open our heart to express our gratitude to God for his abiding presence. We thank him for the gift of the day with all its events and challenges. We thank him for everything we were able to accomplish, and we entrust to God all our concerns for tomorrow.

> From the rising to the setting of the sun,
> may the name of the Lord be praised.
> Glory be to the Father, and to the Son, and to the
> Holy Spirit,
> as it was in the beginning, is now, and will be
> forever. Amen.

Take a few moments for a brief examination of conscience. Reflect on the ways God acted in your life today, consider how you responded to his invitations to think, speak, and act in a Christ-like manner, and in what ways you would like to be a more faithful disciple tomorrow.

You may choose other Psalms of praise and petition from your Bible.

Psalm 67

May God bless us and may all the ends of the earth worship him.

May God be gracious to us and bless us.
    May he let his face shine upon us,
that your ways may be known on earth;
    and your salvation, among all nations.
Let the peoples praise you, O God,
    let all the peoples praise you.
Let the nations sing and shout with joy
    for you judge the peoples with righteousness,
    and guide the nations on the earth.
Let the peoples praise you, O God,
    let all the peoples praise you.
The earth has brought forth its fruit.
    May God, our God, bless us.
May God indeed bless us,
    and may all the ends of the earth revere him.

Glory be . . .

Psalm 18

The Lord lightens my darkness; his promises are true.

The Lord is my stronghold, my fortress, my rescuer,
    my God is my rock where I take refuge.
    He is my shield, my saving power, my strength.
I call on the Lord, worthy of all praise,
    and I am saved from my enemies.
In my distress, I called to the Lord and
    from his temple my God heard my voice;
    my cry came to his presence, to his very ears.
This is why I will praise you, LORD, among the
    nations
    and sing psalms to your name.

Glory be . . .

The Word of God

John 15:4–5, 7

Our routine activities take on deeper meaning when we invite Jesus to abide at the center of our lives. When we recognize and accept the love he offers us, we experience an interior peace that gives way to hope during the difficult times and authentic joy during the good times.

Abide in me, and I will abide in you.
Just as the branch cannot bear fruit on its own
unless it remains on the vine,
Likewise you cannot unless you abide in me.
I am the vine, you are the branches.
Whoever abides in me, and I in him,
He it is who bears much fruit,
For apart from me you can do nothing. . . .
If you abide in me, and my words abide in you,
Ask whatever you wish, and it will happen to you.

*In our evening prayer we entrust our needs and the
needs of our loved ones to the Lord. We take a moment to
consider the needs of the world and intercede for those
who do not or cannot pray. We offer petitions for the
improvement of the human condition so that our world
can be a better place to live, and that all people will contribute to building up God's kingdom here on earth.*

Good and gracious God, we thank you for the gifts
you have given us this day. With confidence in your
loving care, we present to you our needs and the needs
of all your people.

For Church leaders and those who minister in your
name: may they lead lives of holiness and seek to

be true witnesses to the Gospel message of love and compassion.

Response: *Lord, hear our prayer through the intercession of Saint Joseph.*

For world leaders: may they govern with integrity and justice, safeguarding the rights and dignity of all human persons, especially the most vulnerable. R̶.

For those involved in peace efforts throughout the world: may their labors be effective and blessed with God's love. R̶.

For all mothers and fathers: may the Holy Spirit grant them the love, wisdom, and courage they need to form their children as faith-filled disciples of Jesus. R̶.

For the elderly, the homebound, and the terminally ill: may they find comfort in God's love for them and support from compassionate friends and caregivers. R̶.

For the homeless and all those who suffer in body, mind, or spirit: may they experience the kindness and support of the human family and the compassionate touch of the Divine Healer. R̶.

For all who have died: may they soon enjoy light, happiness, and peace in the joy of eternal life. ℟.

(Add your own general and particular intentions.)

Conclude your intercessions by praying to our heavenly Father in the words Jesus taught us:

Our Father, p. 13.

Closing Prayer

Good and gracious Lord, receive our evening prayer. Guard us from evil and grant us a restful sleep, so that with the coming of a new day we may serve you with renewed strength and joy. We ask this in the name of Jesus, your Son. Amen.

Before retiring for the night, it is customary to place ourselves and our loved ones under the protection of our Blessed Mother.

Hail, Holy Queen, p. 20, or the Memorare, p. 21.

Self-Dedication to Saint Joseph

Accept, dear Saint Joseph, the consecration which I now make of myself to you. I dedicate myself wholly to you, that you may always be my father, my protector, and my guide in the way of salvation. Obtain for me purity of heart and sincerity in pursuit of holiness of life. Grant that, following your example, I may direct all my actions to the greater glory of God, in union with the Divine Heart of Jesus, with the Immaculate Heart of Mary, and with you. Finally, pray for me, that I may share in the peace and joy you had at the hour of your holy death. Amen.

To Know One's Vocation in Life

O great Saint Joseph, so docile to the guidance of the Holy Spirit, obtain for me the grace to know the way of life God in his Providence desires for me. Do not let me be deceived regarding so important a decision. My happiness in this life and perhaps even my eternal salvation depends on this choice. Obtain for me the light to know the will of God, to be faithful in carrying it out, and to choose the vocation which will lead me to eternal happiness. Amen.

Consecration to Saint Joseph

I come before you, O glorious Saint Joseph, and venerate you as the chaste spouse of the Mother of God, as the head of the Holy Family, as the foster father of Jesus Christ, as the faithful guardian of the treasures of the Blessed Trinity. In you I venerate the choice of God the Father. He desired to share with you his authority over his eternal, only-begotten Son, who wished to be dependent on you and to owe his well-being to the labor of your hands. In you I venerate the choice of God the Holy Spirit, who wished to entrust to you Mary, his faithful spouse, and to give you to her as her guardian and companion through life.

I honor you for the privilege of being permitted to carry Jesus Christ, the Son of God, in your arms, to hold him close to you, to embrace him lovingly. Who can comprehend the overwhelming treasures of light, wisdom, and grace which you acquired during the time you lived in the company of Jesus and Mary!

Filled with reverence and love when contemplating your greatness and sanctity, I offer and consecrate to you my heart. After Jesus and Mary, you shall be its lord and master. From this day forward I shall consider you as my father and protector. Look upon me as your child. Let me experience the effects of the esteem in which you are held by God, and your tender love toward me who has entrusted myself to your keeping.

Obtain for me a sincere and lasting conversion of heart, with all the graces I need to fulfill the holy will of God. Obtain for me your spirit of interior recollection, your fidelity to grace, your intimate union with God, your profound humility, your patience in trials, your wholehearted devotion to the ways of Divine Providence, and especially your fervent love for the sacred person of Jesus Christ and for Mary, his immaculate Mother: the virtues which constitute your special, immeasurable holiness.

O great saint, take under your protection the devout persons who, following your example, do their best to imitate Jesus and Mary by leading a hidden, secluded life.

Finally, O glorious saint, through the special grace of your holy death in the arms of Jesus and Mary, obtain for me a similar death, with perfect surrender to the will of God, and the assistance of Jesus and Mary. Amen.

Venerable Henri Marie Boudon

For Those in One's Care

Great Saint Joseph, the Son of God-made-man and his most holy Mother the ever-virgin Mary were entrusted to your loving care: hear and answer the prayers I offer to you on behalf of those who have been entrusted to my care and keeping by the same Providence as chose you. Extend to me this grace above all else: that nothing I do or say shall ever obscure the face of God for them or cause them to love God less. Give them the same fatherly love and protection as you gave the Christ Child and his Mother—protect them from harm, preserve them from evil, counsel them in doubt, grant them the joy that is the inheritance of God's children. Through your intercession I am confident that nothing will harm their spiritual growth, that you will guide them safely to maturity and to full stature in Christ Jesus our Lord. Amen.

To Obtain a Special Favor

O glorious Saint Joseph, steadfast follower of Jesus Christ, I am confident that your prayers for me will be graciously heard at the throne of God. To you I lift my heart and hands, asking your powerful intercession to obtain from the compassionate Heart of Jesus all the graces necessary for my spiritual and temporal well-being, particularly the grace of a happy death, and the special grace for which I now pray (*mention your request*).

Saint Joseph, Guardian of the Word Incarnate, by the love you bear for Jesus Christ, and for the glory of his name, hear my prayer and obtain my petitions. Amen.

Daily Prayer for Protection

Great Saint Joseph, you are the faithful protector and intercessor of all who love and honor you. You know that I have special confidence in you, and, after Jesus and Mary, place all my hope of salvation in you, for you are all-powerful with God and will never abandon your faithful devotees. Therefore, I humbly call upon you and entrust myself, all who are dear to me, and all that I possess to your secure protection and powerful intercession. I beseech you, by the love of Jesus and Mary, do not abandon me during life, and assist me at the hour of my death. Amen.

Venerable Martin Von Cochem

In Praise of Saint Joseph

I praise you dear Saint Joseph, man according to the heart of God. You were found worthy to be the husband of the Virgin Mary and foster father of the Son of God. To you God sent an angel to reveal the wondrous mystery of the Incarnation and the plans of his holy will. God bestowed on you countless graces, gave you the privilege of living with Jesus and Mary, sharing their joys and sorrows; patience amidst trials; and perseverance amid the toil of daily labor. With great fidelity you followed every inspiration from heaven, and with full confidence placed yourself in the hands of Divine Providence, grateful for his loving care.

God will also take care of me if I, like you, live according to his holy will, and if like you I make his honor and glory the aim of my life. O Blessed Saint Joseph, may your life be an inspiration to me when I find it hard to be faithful in the practice of virtue and in the fulfillment of my duties. Help me to imitate your example, to trust in God's grace, and to have the great happiness of dying in the friendship of Jesus and under the protection of Mary. Amen.

SAINT JOSEPH

STRENGTH OF FATHERS
AND PILLAR OF FAMILY LIFE

Every child is the bearer of a unique mystery that can only be brought to light with the help of a father who respects that child's freedom. A father who realizes that he is most a father and educator at the point when he becomes "useless," when he sees that his child has become independent and can walk the paths of life unaccompanied. When he becomes like Joseph, who always knew that his child was not his own but had merely been entrusted to his care.

Pope Francis, *Patris Corde*, 7

Introduction

THE VOCATION, OR the calling, of Saint Joseph was to safeguard the well-being of Mary and Jesus by providing for them during the years of our Lord's childhood, adolescence, and early manhood. He was chosen by God to be Mary's spouse, assuring fatherly protection of Jesus as his legal father. Joseph was Mary's husband whom she loved; Mary was Joseph's wife, whom he loved, and the natural mother of Jesus. They were a family who shared the joys, anxieties, misunderstandings, and hardships that all families encounter in their life together.

Granted they were the *Holy* Family, but that doesn't mean they were exempt from the complexities of life. The narratives of Matthew and Luke make general reference to some of those hardships. Filling in the details and imagining the events from Saint Joseph's perspective would make anyone wonder how he did it and why he did it: walking to Bethlehem with a pregnant wife and arriving too late to secure suitable lodging; helping to birth the child, Son of the Most High; rushing off in the middle of the night for Egypt to save the life of the Son of God and living there as refugees; searching for God's Son in Jerusalem when he decided to stay behind to debate with the teachers of the Law.

Saint Joseph knew who he was and what God wanted of him, and that assurance gave him the courage he needed to overcome the obstacles life presented. We can say that Joseph was the Holy Family's rock of strength, the one Mary and Jesus depended on to watch over them. With his examples of loving concern, responsibility, and obedience to God's will, Saint Joseph is a model and patron of fathers and parents who value their vocation and strive to live it with love and dedication.

A Father's Prayer

Saint Joseph, foster father of Jesus, pray for me. Like you, I am a father, provider, protector, mentor, and spouse. Teach me the virtues of trust, prayer, and confidence in God's plan for me and my family. Show me how to form in my children the virtues you instilled in Jesus. Fill me with respect and love for their mother as you loved and respected Mary. Saint Joseph, pray for me and for all fathers. Amen.

For One's Family

Heavenly Father, I thank you for the gift of my family and for the many joys and blessings that have come to me through each of them. Help me to appreciate the uniqueness of each while celebrating the diversity of all. Through the intercession of Saint Joseph, foster father of your Son, I ask you to protect my family from the evils of this world. Grant us all the power to forgive when we have been hurt and the humility to ask forgiveness when we have caused pain. Unite us in the love of your Son, Jesus, so that we may be a sign of the unity you desire for all humanity. And at life's end, may we together attain heaven where we will praise and thank you for all eternity. Saint Joseph, intercede for us. Amen.

In Time of Difficulty

Holy Joseph, with heartfelt confidence I come before you to seek your compassion and support. With fatherly care you accompanied and protected Jesus during his childhood. With the love and devotion of a spouse you cherished Mary his Mother. Now, in your kindness, I ask your help in this time of difficulty. By the love you had for Jesus and Mary on earth, I ask you to calm my distress and present my petition to our heavenly Father (*mention your request*).

Lord, give me the spirit of Saint Joseph so that even amid my own hardships I can look beyond myself and reach out to others who are alone and suffering and thus be an instrument of your love and compassion. Amen.

For Guidance

O glorious Saint Joseph, guardian and protector of the Holy Family, in your kindness teach me the way to integrity of mind and heart, humility of spirit, and dedication to faith-filled abandonment to the divine will. Be a father to me throughout life: my guide, my protector, my model, that I may one day merit to die as you did in the arms of Jesus and Mary. Amen.

For Every Need

Be mindful of us, O blessed Joseph; plead our cause before your foster Son, Jesus. Intercede on our behalf with the Blessed Virgin Mary, your spouse, the Mother of him, who with the Father and the Holy Spirit lives and reigns world without end. Amen.

Saint Bernardine of Siena

A Father's Prayer for His Children

Saint Joseph, you were the foster father of Jesus and taught the Son of God everything from virtues to woodworking to how to pray. You protected him from harm, found him when he was lost, and provided for him as he grew up. Teach me how to be a good father. Show me how to practice and teach my children the virtues of faith, hope, and love, courage, obedience, and love for the poor. As they grow up and choose their direction in life, lead me in giving them good advice. Let my children see me praying and give me the courage and confidence to pray with them. Protect my children from harm as you once protected Jesus from the threats of Herod. Help me preserve my job so that I can provide for them and teach them the value of honest work and trust in Divine Providence. Saint Joseph, patron of fathers, pray for me. Amen.

Strangers in a Foreign Land

Lord God, help us to remember those who tonight will go to sleep unfed and unwelcome, strangers in foreign lands, people who have fled for their lives and are far from their homes. We lift up to you those who are escaping persecution and conflict, having fled death, torture, or ruthless exploitation. So many carry wounds, mental and physical. So many have suffered greatly.

Lord Jesus, give us more of your compassion for their plight, soften our hearts to their situation, and help us follow your lead in seeking justice and mercy on their behalf. We pray for an end to the wars, poverty, and human rights abuses that drive desperate people to become refugees in the first place. We give thanks for people working in troubled countries and ask for more of your blessing so we can bring life, dignity, and hope to those that remain.

We thank you that you are Lord of all the earth and all its people are loved by you. We pray these things in the name of your Son who was himself born into the troubled life of a refugee.

Saint Joseph, protector of refugees, intercede for us.

Author Unknown

Novena for Families

THE CATHOLIC TRADITION of praying novenas finds its origin in the earliest days of the Church. It is based on the passage from the Acts of the Apostles, 1:12–14, when, after the Lord's Ascension, the apostles, together with other followers of Jesus, and Mary, his Mother, gathered for nine days in prayer awaiting the coming of the Holy Spirit. This prayer of the first Christian community was the first "novena." The word "novena" derives from the Latin term *novum*, meaning nine. A novena can be prayed solemnly in a parish church, privately in a prayer group, or in the familiarity of your own home. As Christians we never really pray alone. We are members of the body of Christ and are united to every other member of Christ's Mystical Body. When we pray, we are spiritually united with all the other members.

There are various types of novenas, but their purpose is the same: to call to mind our needs, to ask God's help and protection, and to thank the Lord for the graces and blessings we have already received. A novena is a way to respond to Jesus' invitation: "Ask! and it shall be given to you" (Lk 11:9).

How to Pray this Novena: For nine consecutive days, try to set apart a time for reflection on the theme of the day. Pray the Opening Prayer, then read and ponder the Scripture passage, allowing the transforming power of God's word to penetrate your mind and heart. Conclude with an Our Father, Hail Mary, Glory Be, and the Closing Prayer.

For each day:

Opening Prayer

Heavenly Father, you have promised to be with us always. Enlighten, comfort, and provide for all families that they may know you are present in their midst. May family members embrace the good that each member offers so that every home may be a place of harmony and love. Living in acceptance and respect for one another, may families be for the world a witness of your never-failing love.

Through the intercession of Saint Joseph, Guardian of the Holy Family, I ask (*mention your request*), and that you protect my family from the evils of this world. Grant us the power to forgive when we have been hurt and the humility to ask forgiveness when we have caused pain. Unite us in the love of your Son, Jesus, who lives and reigns with you in the unity of the Holy Spirit, one God forever and ever. Amen.

Closing Prayer

Lord our God, thank you for this time of prayer and for the many blessings you continue to bestow on us through your goodness and love. I pray that all families may truly be a place of unity, love, and belonging. Heal our brokenness, bind our wounds, increase our patience and mercy so that we may live in peace of mind and heart. Amen.

Saint Joseph, intercede for us.

———◈———

Day One

Our Family Comes from God

Pray opening prayer, p. 55.

For meditation

The Lord God said, "It is not good that the man should be alone; I will make him a helper as his partner." So the Lord God caused a deep sleep to fall upon the man, and he slept; then he took one of his ribs and closed up its place with flesh. And the rib that the Lord God had taken from the man he made into a woman and brought her to the man. Then the man said, "This at last is bone of my bones and flesh of my flesh; this one shall be called Woman, for out of Man this one was taken." Therefore a man leaves his father and his mother and clings to his wife, and they become one flesh.

Gen 2:18, 21–24

For reflection

God's plan is for my family to live in loving communion, like the three Persons of the Trinity. What can I do to better realize this and act accordingly?

Pray an Our Father, Hail Mary, and Glory Be.
Pray closing prayer, p. 56.

Day Two

Families Thrive
on Mutual Respect and Love

Pray opening prayer, p. 55.

For meditation

Be subject to one another out of reverence for Christ.

Eph 5:21

This is a tremendous mystery. I am applying it to Christ and the church, but each one of you should in the same way love his wife as he loves himself, and the wife should respect her husband.

Eph 5:32–33

"I give you a new commandment—love one another. As I have loved you, you too should love one another. All will know by this that you are my disciples, if you have love for one another."

Jn 13:34–35

For reflection

My family is like a school where each member learns to love and respect others through practice, effort, and example. How well do I teach and learn in this school?

Pray an Our Father, Hail Mary, and Glory Be.
Pray closing prayer, p. 56.

DAY THREE

Cherish Each Family Member

Pray opening prayer, p. 55.

For meditation

Faithful friends are a sturdy shelter:
> whoever finds one has found a treasure.

Faithful friends are beyond price;
> no amount can balance their worth.

Faithful friends are lifesaving medicine;
> and those who fear the Lord will find them.

Those who fear the Lord direct their friendship aright,
> for as they are, so are their neighbors also.

Sir 6:14–17

For reflection

Each member of my family, even those who are difficult, is a true gift from God, unique and unrepeatable. How can I better live out this conviction?

Pray an Our Father, Hail Mary, and Glory Be.
Pray closing prayer, p. 56.

Day Four

Children, Honor Your Parents

Pray opening prayer, p. 55.

For meditation

> Listen to me your father, O children;
>> act accordingly, that you may be kept in safety.
> For the Lord honors a father above his children,
>> and he confirms a mother's right over her children.
> Those who honor their father atone for sins,
>> and those who respect their mother are like those
>>> who lay up treasure.
> Those who respect their father will have long life,
>> and those who honor their mother obey the Lord.
>
> *Sir 3:1–4, 6*

For reflection

In what ways do I show respect, kindness, and consideration to my parents?

Pray an Our Father, Hail Mary, and Glory Be.
Pray closing prayer, p. 56.

Day Five

Parents, Imitate God's Love

Pray opening prayer, p. 55.

For meditation

> When Israel was a child, I loved him,
>> and out of Egypt I called my son.
>
> The more I called them,
>> the more they went from me. . . .
>
> Yet it was I who taught Ephraim to walk,
>> I took them up in my arms;
>> But they did not know that I healed them.
>
> I led them with cords of human kindness,
>> with bands of love.
>
> I was to them like those
>> who lift infants to their cheeks.
>> I bent down to them and fed them. . . .
>
> How can I give you up, Ephraim?
>> How can I hand you over, O Israel? . . .
>
> My heart recoils within me;
>> my compassion grows warm and tender.
>
> I will not execute my fierce anger . . .
>> for I am God . . . the Holy One in your midst.

Hos 11:1–4, 8–9

For reflection

Consider that children are introduced to God's love through the self-giving love of their parents. How well do I mirror this love?

Pray an Our Father, Hail Mary, and Glory Be.
Pray closing prayer, p. 56.

Day Six

Family Life Sometimes Requires Sacrifice

Pray opening prayer, p. 55.

For meditation

"Remain in my love. If you keep my commandments, you will remain in my love, just as I have kept my Father's commandments and remain in his love. . . .

"This is my commandment: love one another as I love you. No one has greater love than this, to lay down one's life for one's friends. You are my friends if you do what I command you . . . It was not you who chose me, but I who chose you and appointed you to go and bear fruit that will remain, so that whatever you ask the Father in my name he may give you. This I command you: love one another."

Jn 15:9b–10, 12–14, 16–17 NABRE

For reflection

What sacrifices are being asked of me right now? How is my love for my family responding to these challenges?

Pray an Our Father, Hail Mary, and Glory Be.
Pray closing prayer, p. 56.

We Are Rooted Together in Christ's Love

Pray opening prayer, p. 55.

For meditation

I bend my knees to the Father. From him every family in the heavens and on earth is named, so that from the riches of his glory he may grant you inner strength and power through his Spirit. May Christ dwell in your hearts through faith, firmly rooted and established in love, so that with all the saints you may be able to understand the breadth, the length, the height, and the depth, and know Christ's love which surpasses all knowledge.

Eph 3:14–19

For reflection

When there are tensions, misunderstandings, or estrangements in my family, how do I rely on the love of Christ to bring reconciliation?

Pray an Our Father, Hail Mary, and Glory Be.
Pray closing prayer, p. 56.

DAY EIGHT

God's Powerful Love Saves Us

Pray opening prayer, p. 55.

For meditation

If God is for us, who can be against us? If God did not spare his own Son but instead gave him up for all of us, will he not also freely give us everything along with his Son? Who will accuse God's chosen ones? God himself pardons them! Who will condemn them? Christ died and rose for us and is now at God's right hand interceding for us! Who will separate us from Christ's love? Affliction, distress, persecution, famine, destitution, danger, or the sword? . . . But in all these things we are winning an overwhelming victory through the One who loved us. I am convinced that neither death nor life, neither angels not principalities, neither things present nor to come nor powers, neither height nor depth nor any other created being will be able to separate us from God's love in Christ Jesus our Lord.

Rm 8:31–35, 37–39

For reflection

Whenever I feel afraid for my family, I will recall the power of Christ, who is stronger than any danger we face.

Pray an Our Father, Hail Mary, and Glory Be.
Pray closing prayer, p. 56.

Day Nine

Our Family Has a Mission

Pray opening prayer, p. 55.

For meditation

> They continued to meet daily in the Temple, and at home they broke bread, sharing their food with joy and simplicity of heart, praising God and enjoying the good will of all the people. And day by day the Lord increased the number of those who were being saved.
>
> *Acts 2:46–47*

For reflection

How is my family a witness of the good news of Jesus, by word and example?

Pray an Our Father, Hail Mary, and Glory Be.
Pray closing prayer, p. 56.

SAINT JOSEPH

MODEL OF WORKERS AND
PATRON OF DIVINE PROVIDENCE

Let us think again of Saint Joseph in his poverty and hard work, all his energy engaged in the effort of earning something to live on, and let us then remember that economic goods are indeed worthy of our Christian interest, on condition that they do not become ends in themselves, but are understood and used as means to keep going life which is directed towards other and higher goods, on condition that economic goods are not sought after with greedy egoism, but be rather a source and stimulus of provident charity, on condition again that they be not used as authorization for soft and easy indulgence in the so-called pleasures of life but rather be used for the broad and honest interests of the common good.

Saint Paul VI,
*Homily on the Feast of
Saint Joseph*, 1969

Introduction

SCRIPTURE TELLS US that Saint Joseph was a carpenter, and according to the custom of the time he taught Jesus that same trade. When we think about Jesus, too often we might focus only on his divinity and forget the ways he shared our humanity. Jesus spent his adolescence and early adult life (approximately thirty years of the thirty-three years he lived on earth!) working with Saint Joseph and learning the skills of carpentry. From the example of his foster father he would have also learned the value of hard work and diligence, making beautiful and useful things with his hands.

Saint Joseph provided for Jesus and Mary through the work of his hands, using the talents he had received from God and the skills he had acquired. He exemplifies the ideal of dignified work that not only secures a means of support for a family, but also contributes to the common good.

To work with integrity, with dignity, and with peace of mind, is no easy task. We face difficulties, fatigue, and, at times, a lack of interest in our work or frustration with co-workers. We struggle to work in a way that truly honors God. Saint Joseph can teach us how to make our daily labor a productive offering of praise and gratitude to God.

He was given the task of caring for and watching over the Virgin Mary and acting as father to Jesus, God's Son incarnate. He was certainly aware of his human inability to fill this role, but he trusted in Divine Providence and did everything he was asked to do, to the best of his ability, knowing that the results depended on God. It can be the same for us. We can use our talents and abilities in our daily labor, do our best to act as committed followers of Jesus, and leave the results to God. Pray to Saint Joseph; ask him for this favor.

A Worker's Prayer

Saint Joseph, example for all who work to support themselves and their families, obtain for me the grace to labor with gratitude and joy. Grant that I may consider my job as an opportunity to use and develop the gifts of nature and grace I have received from God. In the workplace may I mirror your virtues of integrity, moderation, patience and inner peace, treating my co-workers with kindness and respect. May all I do and say lead others to the Lord and bring honor to God's name. Amen.

For Someone Seeking Employment

Saint Joseph, foster father of Jesus and spouse of the Virgin Mary, help me to find suitable work, with an adequate salary and essential health benefits. You know the anxiety that I feel as I search for a means to support myself and those who depend on me. I am confident that you understand my need to pay my just debts with dignity, and to help others who are also in need.

Holy Joseph, saint of Divine Providence, teach me to trust in God as a loving Father, and intercede to God for me in all my needs. Amen.

To Saint Joseph, the Worker

The following prayer to Saint Joseph, composed by Saint Pius X, acknowledges the dignity of work and urges us to offer our daily labors to God as a sacrifice. Praying for a good and holy workday can help us turn our daily toil into a gift pleasing to the Lord.

Glorious Saint Joseph, model of all who are engaged in manual labor, obtain for me the grace to work conscientiously, putting the call of duty above my natural inclinations, to work with gratitude and joy, in a spirit of penance for the remission of my sins, considering it an honor to employ and develop by means of labor the gifts received from God, to work with order, peace, moderation, and patience, without cowering from weariness or difficulties, to work above all with purity of intention and detachment from self, thinking of death and the account that I must render of time lost, of talents wasted, of good omitted, of worthless gratification in success, so fatal to the work of God. All for Jesus, all through Mary, all after your example, O holy Joseph. Such shall be my motto in life and in death. Amen.

Saint Pius X

Prayer for Those Who Work

O glorious Saint Joseph,
remind all who work
that they are not alone
in their labor, their joy,
or their sufferings,
because Jesus is by our side,
with Mary, his mother and ours,
supporting them,
wiping sweat from their brow,
and setting a value on their toil.
Teach them to use their labor,
as you did, as a supreme means
of attaining holiness. Amen.

Saint John XXIII

In Time of Financial Need

Saint Joseph, provider for the Holy Family and saint of Divine Providence, I turn to you in my present financial need with confidence and trust, knowing that the goodness and generosity of your heart is constant and unchanging. On earth you mirrored the heavenly

Father's concern and care for Jesus and Mary. Help me provide now for those I love.

You followed the voice of God, moving forward with faith even when all was dark and uncertain. Give me, too, a heart open to God's call and a faith like yours that can look at the present situation with courage, hope, and the certainty that God will provide. Amen.

A Family's Prayer in Time of Need

Saint Joseph, we honor you and call upon you as the protector and provider of the Holy Family, friend of the poor and of those struggling financially to support their families, the saint of Divine Providence. On earth you represented the universal goodness and concern of the heavenly Father. Your life was one of hard work and moderation. Intercede for us as we bring our financial needs to you; present them to the Father and to your foster Son.

We are confident in your intercession and ask that you grant us the wisdom to make practical choices when it comes to living with moderation—to avoid wasting food and clothing, to be content with the good things we have, to learn to do without what is really not needed, to share with those who are less fortunate than we, and to place greater trust in Divine Providence.

Blessed Joseph, we trust that if we do our best to live in moderation, our heavenly Father will not fail to provide for the needs of our family. Strengthen us in our good resolutions, do not allow us to be overcome by anxiety but inspire us with workable solutions during our time of need. We ask this and all things in the name of Jesus. Amen.

Adapted from a prayer
by Blessed James Alberione

To Sell a House or Property

Saint Joseph is commonly known as the patron saint of those wishing to sell their house. There is a tradition of burying a statue of Saint Joseph on the property you wish to sell, but it is not necessary to bury or even buy a statue. One simply asks the intercession of Saint Joseph with faith. If you do have a statue, instead of burying it, you can place it in your house as a reminder to pray to Saint Joseph. When the house sells and you move, bring the statue with you and place it in a prominent area of the house in gratitude for his assistance.

Dear Saint Joseph, help me to sell this house and property quickly. I ask you to intercede for me with the heavenly Father for this grace. I ask also for prudence, that I may make wise decisions regarding this sale and that the proceeds will be sufficient to sustain me with my future needs.

Saint Joseph, foster father of Jesus and husband of Mary, ask the Lord to bless my family and the memories that were made here. May this house and property continue to be a home that nurtures love and peace. Amen.

To Find a New Home

As Guardian of the Holy Family, Saint Joseph was responsible for finding a house for Jesus and Mary to live in while on earth. Over time he has become known for his heavenly assistance in securing a home for those who place their trust in his intercession.

Dear Saint Joseph, intercede for me with the heavenly Father, that I might find a new home for my family. We are in need of a house that is adequate for our needs and in an area that is safe for my family. I know you understand the urgency of my request and the anxieties that accompany my search. You and Mary were forced to leave your home in Nazareth and travel to Bethlehem where you had difficulty in finding lodging for your pregnant wife. To save the Son of God from Herod's wrath, you were forced to leave your homeland; you took refuge in a land amid a culture and religion unknown to you, and patiently waited for the death of Herod before returning to Nazareth with Jesus and Mary. Saint Joseph, help me to be patient and to trust that in due time God will provide for the needs of my family. Amen.

Novena to Find Employment

THE CATHOLIC TRADITION of praying novenas finds its origin in the earliest days of the Church. It is based on the passage from the Acts of the Apostles, 1:12–14, when, after the Lord's Ascension, the apostles, together with other followers of Jesus, and Mary, his Mother, gathered for nine days in prayer awaiting the coming of the Holy Spirit. This prayer of the first Christian community was the first "novena." The word "novena" derives from the Latin term *novum*, meaning nine. A novena can be prayed solemnly in a parish church, privately in a prayer group, or in the familiarity of your own home. As Christians we never really pray alone. We are members of the body of Christ and are united to every other member of Christ's Mystical Body. When we pray, we are spiritually united with all the other members.

There are various types of novenas, but their purpose is the same: to call to mind our needs, to ask God's help and protection, and to thank the Lord for the graces and blessings we have already received. A novena is a way to respond to Jesus' invitation: "Ask! and it shall be given to you" (Lk 11:9).

How to Pray this Novena: For nine consecutive days, try to set apart a time for reflection on the theme of the day. Pray the Opening Prayer, then read and ponder the Scripture passage, allowing the transforming power of God's word to penetrate your mind and heart. Conclude with an Our Father, Hail Mary, Glory Be, and the Closing Prayer.

For each day:

Opening Prayer

O God, Creator of the universe, in every age you call us to develop and use our natural gifts for the good of others. Through human work you continually perfect and direct your work of creation. Listen to the prayers of your people and grant to everyone employment that ennobles and elevates, so that all who work may have secure employment and a fitting standard of living. *(Mention your specific request.)*

By the example of Saint Joseph, and under his patronage, inspire us to walk always in your way of holiness. With Saint Joseph as our model and guide, grant that we may serve our brothers and sisters through our work and come to the rewards you have promised. We ask this through your Son, our Lord Jesus Christ, in the unity of the Holy Spirit, one God forever and ever. Amen.

Closing Prayer

Thank you, Lord, for this time of prayer for my loved ones and for myself. I am confident that with your grace I will find suitable and dignified work. Through my work I will participate in your creation, fulfill my calling, support my family, and help build up your kingdom here on earth, a society of brothers and sisters, united together as your children. Through your Son, our Lord Jesus Christ, in the unity of the Holy Spirit, one God forever and ever. Amen.

Saint Joseph, intercede for us.

Day One

We Are the Work of God

Pray opening prayer, p. 83.

For meditation

In the beginning when God created the heavens and the earth, the earth was a formless void and darkness covered the face of the deep, while a wind from God swept over the face of the waters. God saw everything that he had made, and indeed, it was very good.

Gen 1:1–2, 31

Yet, O Lord, you are our Father; we are the clay, and you are our potter; we are all the work of your hand.

Is 64:8

In the beginning was the Word,
    and the Word was with God,
    and the Word was God.
He was in the beginning with God.
All things came to be through him,
    and without him nothing came to be.

Jn 1:1–3

To recall throughout the day

"But first seek the Kingdom and the will of God and all those things will be given to you also."

Mt 6:33

Pray an Our Father, Hail Mary, and Glory Be.
Pray closing prayer, p. 84.

Day Two

Our Work Accomplishes Nothing Without God

Pray opening prayer, p. 83.

For meditation

"I am the vine, you are the branches. Whoever abides in me, and I in him, he it is who bears much fruit, for apart from me you can do nothing."

Jn 15:5

If it is not the LORD who builds a house,
  Its builders strain at it to no purpose.
If it is not the LORD who guards a city,
  Guards keep watch to no purpose.

Ps 127:1

After he had finished speaking, he said to Simon, "Put out into deep water and lower your nets for a catch." Simon said in reply, "Master, we have worked hard all night and have caught nothing, but at your command I will lower the nets." When they had done this, they caught a great number of fish and their nets were tearing.

Lk 5:4–6, NABRE

To recall throughout the day

"But first seek the Kingdom and the will of God and all those things will be given to you also."

Mt 6:33

Pray an Our Father, Hail Mary, and Glory Be.
Pray closing prayer, p. 84.

Day Three

We are Fulfilled as Human Beings Through Work

Pray opening prayer, p. 83.

For meditation

Then God said, Let us make human beings in our image, after our likeness. Let them have dominion over the fish of the sea, the birds of the air, the tame animals, all the wild animals, and all the creatures that crawl on the earth.

God created mankind in his image;
in the image of God he created them;
male and female he created them.

God blessed them and God said to them: Be fertile and multiply; fill the earth and subdue it. Have dominion over the fish of the sea, the birds of the air, and all the living things that crawl on the earth.

Gen 1:26–28, NABRE

The Lord God then took the man and settled him in the garden of Eden, to cultivate and care for it.

Gen 2:15, NABRE

To recall throughout the day

"But first seek the Kingdom and the will of God and all those things will be given to you also."

Mt 6:33

Pray an Our Father, Hail Mary, and Glory Be.
Pray closing prayer, p. 84.

Day Four

Our Work Should Be for the Glory of God

Pray opening prayer, p. 83.

For meditation

"Let your light shine before others, so that they may
see your good works and give glory to your Father in
heaven."

Mt 5:16, NRSV

Whether you eat or drink or whatever you do, do
everything for the glory of God.

1 Cor 10:31 NRSV

Whatever you do, let it be from the heart, as if you
were working for the Lord rather than for men, in
the knowledge that as your reward you will receive
an inheritance from the Lord.

Col 3:23–24

Render service with enthusiasm, as to the Lord and
not to men and women, knowing that whatever

good we do, we will receive the same again from the Lord.

Eph 6:7–8, NRSV

To recall throughout the day

"But first seek the Kingdom and the will of God and all those things will be given to you also."

Mt 6:33

Pray an Our Father, Hail Mary, and Glory Be.
Pray closing prayer, p. 84.

Day Five

God Wants Us to Live Balanced Lives

Pray opening prayer, p. 83.

For meditation

For everything there is a season, and a time for every
matter under heaven:

a time to be born, and a time to die;

a time to plant, and a time to pluck up what is
planted;

a time to kill, and a time to heal;

a time to break down, and a time to build up;

a time to weep, and a time to laugh;

a time to mourn, and a time to dance;

a time to throw away stones, and a time to gather
stones together.

Eccles 3:1–5

On the seventh day God finished the work that he
had done, and he rested on the seventh day from all
the work that he had done. So God blessed the seventh day and hallowed it, because on it God rested
from all the work that he had done in creation.

Gen 2:2–3

Six days you shall labor and do all your work. But the seventh day is a sabbath to the Lord your God; you shall not do any work.

Ex 20:9–10

To recall throughout the day

"But first seek the Kingdom and the will of God and all those things will be given to you also."

Mt 6:33

Pray an Our Father, Hail Mary, and Glory Be.
Pray closing prayer, p. 84.

Day Six

God Wants Our Work to Uplift Others

Pray opening prayer, p. 83.

For meditation

"Whoever obeys and teaches the commandments, he shall be called great in the Kingdom of heaven."

Mt 5:19

Whatever you do, whether in word or deed, do it all in the name of Jesus the Lord, and give thanks to God the Father through him.

Col 3:17

To recall throughout the day

"But first seek the Kingdom and the will of God and all those things will be given to you also."

Mt 6:33

Pray an Our Father, Hail Mary, and Glory Be.
Pray closing prayer, p. 84.

Day Seven

Our Work Builds Up God's World

Pray opening prayer, p. 83.

For meditation

So it is with the smith, sitting by the anvil,
Intent on his iron-work;
the breath of the fire melts his flesh,
and he struggles with the heat of the furnace;
the sound of the hammer deafens his ears,
and his eyes are on the pattern of the object.
He sets his heart on finishing his handiwork,
and he is careful to complete its decoration.
All these [workers] rely on their hands,
and all are skillful in their own work.
Without them no city can be inhabited,
and wherever they live, they will not go hungry. . . .
they cannot expound discipline or judgment,
and they are not found among the rulers.
But they maintain the fabric of the world,
and their concern is for the exercise of their trade.

Sir 38:28, 31–34

To recall throughout the day

"But first seek the Kingdom and the will of God and all those things will be given to you also."

Mt 6:33

Pray an Our Father, Hail Mary, and Glory Be.
Pray closing prayer on p. 84.

DAY EIGHT

Let Us Unite Our Work
to the Wondrous Work of God

Pray opening prayer, p. 83.

For meditation

> When I look at your heavens, the work of your fingers,
> the moon and the stars that you have established;
> what are human beings that you are mindful of them . . . ?

Ps 8:3–4, NRSV

> Praise the LORD! . . .
> Great are the works of the LORD,
>   studied by all who delight in them.
> Full of honor and majesty is his work,
> and his righteousness endures forever.

Ps 111:1–3, NRSV

To recall throughout the day

> "But first seek the Kingdom and the will of God and
> all those things will be given to you also."

Mt 6:33

Pray an Our Father, Hail Mary, and Glory Be.
Pray closing prayer, p. 84.

Day Nine

Let Us Surrender Our Work and Burdens to God

Pray opening prayer, p. 83.

For meditation

I relieved your shoulder of the burden;
>   your hands were freed from the basket.
In distress you called, and I rescued you;
>   I answered you in the secret place of thunder.

Ps 81:6–7, NRSV

"Come to me, all you who labor and are burdened,
and I will give you rest. Take my yoke upon you and
learn from me, for I am meek and humble of heart;
and you will find rest for yourselves. For my yoke is
easy, and my burden light."

Mt 11:28–30, NABRE

To recall throughout the day

"But first seek the Kingdom and the will of God and
all those things will be given to you also."

Mt 6:33

Pray an Our Father, Hail Mary, and Glory Be.
Pray closing prayer, p. 84.

TERROR OF DEMONS

What valor and strength did [Joseph] not display in the victory which he gained over the two greatest enemies of man, the devil and the world? And that by the practice of a most perfect humility, as we have said, throughout the whole course of his life. . . . Valiant and strong is the one who, like Saint Joseph, perseveres in humility; he will be conqueror at once of the devil and of the world, which is full of ambition, vanity, and pride.

Saint Francis de Sales

Introduction

NONE OF US is completely free from sin and temptation. Even Jesus, who was sinless, was tempted by Satan, so we should not be surprised to face temptations. We need God's help to be able to resist the devil's assault and overcome these trials. We need to pray regularly and fervently for guidance and deliverance from spiritual dangers that can easily ensnare us. There is no denying that the powers of evil and darkness are roaming about the earth seeking to draw us into sin and spiritual ruin.

Saint Joseph was chosen by God to be the guardian of the Holy Family, the one who would protect Mary and Jesus from earthly dangers (Mt 2:13–15, 19–23). Just as Saint Joseph protected the Holy Family from the powers of evil, he can protect us on our earthly pilgrimage to heaven. We can call upon Saint Joseph as our spiritual defender and powerful intercessor against spiritual evils.

He is given the title *Terror of Demons* primarily because when someone calls upon him for help against the forces of evil, he becomes their powerful advocate against the hidden strategies of Satan, shedding light on his duplicity and deception. This humble and quiet man of strength sows extreme fear among the powers of darkness because he offers hope and guidance to those who call upon him in their time of need. Be assured that you are not alone in your daily battle. Saint Joseph is ready and able to help defeat your spiritual enemies.

For Protection

Great Saint Joseph,
You were the guardian of our Lord, Jesus Christ,
in his boyhood and young manhood,
and he called you his father.
Be a father to me,
since Jesus has made himself my brother.
You labored for him; taught him to work.
Teach me, too.
You kept him safe during the flight into Egypt;
keep me safe in my journey through life.
Grant that I may never turn aside from the right
    path
of the love of our Lord,
and of faith, and hope in him.
May I, as you did,
have Jesus and Mary at my deathbed;
and, as you are now,
may I be united with them forever in heaven.
    Amen.

In Time of Need

Saint Joseph, patron of all who serve God in simplicity of heart and steadfast devotion, ask the Lord to fill my heart with the fire of his love. Awaken within me the virtues of integrity, reverence, and kindness, so that I may radiate God's love to everyone around me. Intercede for me in my time of particular need and obtain for me the favor I ask (*mention your request*). Blessed Joseph, defend me against the forces of evil that lay in wait at every turn, be my protector in life and my consoler at the moment of death. Amen.

For Defense against the Powers of Evil

Saint Joseph, defender against the powers of evil, with your mighty staff protect us against the devil and his minions. With Jesus and Mary you fled through the night to avoid the wicked designs of Herod; now through the power of God, strike out against the evil spirits that try to ensnare the followers of Jesus Christ. Grant special protection, we pray, for children, parents, families, for priests and religious and the dying. By God's grace, no demon dares approach while you are near, so we implore you, always be near to us! Amen.

To Lead a Virtuous Life

Saint Joseph, my loving father, I place myself forever under your protection. Look on me as your child and keep me from all sin. I take refuge in your arms, so that you may lead me along the path of virtue and assist me at the hour of my death.

Saint Clement Mary Hofbauer, CSsR

For the Conversion of a Loved One

It is well to recall that it is God who ultimately moves the heart of a person to conversion. While we can confidently invoke the intercession of Saint Joseph and pray continually for our loved ones, the conversion of heart and mind of another is God's domain.

Saint Joseph, who throughout the ages is called a "just and holy" man, I urgently recommend to you the conversion of (*N.*) whom Jesus redeemed at the price of his precious blood. You know how empty and unhappy are the lives of those who dismiss our loving Savior from their hearts, and how they expose themselves to the danger of losing him for all eternity. I beg you to intercede for (*N.*) who is so dear to me and is living far from God. Preserve him/her from danger. Ask our Lord Jesus Christ to touch the heart of this wayward soul and lead him/her back to God. Do not abandon him/her until the gates of the heavenly city have been opened to him/her where he/she will praise, bless, and thank God throughout eternity for the graces owed to your powerful intercession. Amen.

For Non-Practicing Catholics

Lord Jesus Christ, let the light of eternal truth shine upon the minds of those who no longer practice their Catholic faith (*mention names*). Clear away the clouds of error and prejudice from their eyes that they may once again wholeheartedly accept and embrace the teachings of your Church. Unite them to yourself in the sacraments of your love, and grant that, sharing in the blessings of your grace in this life, they may come at last to enjoy the eternal reward which you have promised to all those who believe in you. Through the intercession of Saint Joseph, your beloved foster father, hear this my petition, O merciful Jesus, who with the Father and the Holy Spirit, live and reign forever and ever. Amen.

Invocations for Deliverance

O Blood and Water, which poured forth from the Heart of Jesus as a fount of mercy for us, I trust in you.

O my God, free me from every evil of mind, heart, spirit, and body that I may enjoy your peace always, in the name of Jesus Christ, our Lord. Amen.

Pope Sixtus V had this short prayer engraved into the base of the obelisk erected in Saint Peter's Square in Rome. Also called the "motto of Saint Anthony," this invocation can be prayed to overcome any temptations we face.

English:

Behold, the Cross of the Lord!
Be gone, all evil powers!
The Lion of the tribe of Judah,
The Root of David, has conquered!
Alleluia, Alleluia!

Latin:

Ecce Crucem Domini!
Fugite partes adversae!
Vicit Leo de tribu Juda,
Radix David!
Alleluia!

SAINT JOSEPH

GUARDIAN OF PURITY

Marriage and virginity are two ways of expressing and living the one mystery of the Covenant of God with his people, the Covenant which is a communion of love between God and human beings. Through his complete self-sacrifice, Joseph expressed his generous love for the Mother of God and gave her a husband's "gift of self." Even though he decided to draw back so as not to interfere in the plan of God which was coming to pass in Mary, Joseph obeyed the explicit command of the angel and took Mary into his home, while respecting the fact that she belonged exclusively to God.

Saint John Paul II,
Guardian of the Redeemer, 20

Introduction

You probably have seen paintings of the birth of Jesus in which Joseph looks like an old man. This was a common depiction of him in times past, in an effort to uphold the virginity of Mary and the virgin birth of Jesus in an unambiguous way. However, as was said before, it is likely that Joseph was a very young man at the time of his betrothal to Mary. Mary's perpetual virginity was not due to Joseph's old age, but to the reverence Joseph had for Mary and for the mystery of her total belonging to God.

Saint Joseph is a model of purity for us today. We can look to the example of his pure and tender love for Mary and his self-mastery for inspiration in our own struggles. Saint Joseph can help us see in ourselves and in everyone we meet the very image of God, which calls us to respect, reverence, and love each person, and never to use them.

We can turn to the fatherly heart of Saint Joseph for understanding and encouragement, especially in moments of struggle or failure. And he is a powerful intercessor against the forces of darkness that want to lead us along the path of spiritual decay. Saint Joseph devoted himself to everything God asked of him. Through his daily efforts and actions, Joseph gave an ongoing "yes" to God and accepted the opportunity to share in God's divine plan. In Saint Joseph was fulfilled the promise of Jesus: "Blessed are the pure in heart for they shall see God" (Mt 5:8).

Daily Offering

Receive me, Saint Joseph, and the offering of this day through the Sacred Hearts of Jesus and Mary. I offer all my prayers, works, joys, and sufferings to Jesus Christ in reparation for my sins, for the salvation of all my dear ones and the intentions of our Holy Father. Grant that today, my thoughts, words, and actions may be pure and pleasing to the Divine Majesty, and that all I do and say will be accepted by God as an act of love for his honor and glory. Amen.

For Purity of Mind and Heart

Saint Joseph, father and guardian of virgins, into your faithful keeping God entrusted Christ Jesus and Mary, the Virgin of virgins. I beseech you through Jesus and Mary, who were so dear to you, to keep me free from all sin. Grant that my mind be untainted, my heart pure and my body chaste; help me always to serve Jesus and Mary in perfect chastity. Amen.

Act of Entrustment

Saint Joseph, faithful guardian of the Holy Family, your most chaste heart was always in tune with the Divine Heart and surrendered to the divine will of the Father. Like Jesus and Mary, I entrust myself to your pure and vigilant heart for protection, and I place myself and those I love under your guardianship. Protect us from evil. Teach us to love and obey the will of God and to live our lives in the company of Jesus and Mary.

Hearts of Jesus, Mary, and Joseph, I trust in you!

For Moments of Temptation

O Saint Joseph, most chaste guardian of the Holy
Family, be my guardian now.
Defend my mind, that I may only contemplate
what is pure and holy.
Defend my heart, that I may desire only the good.
Defend my will, that I may choose only the love of
Jesus. Amen.

For Holiness of Life

O holy Joseph, I give thanks to God for the many graces bestowed on you, and I ask your intercession to help me persevere in the practice of virtue. Pray for me, O great saint, that I may imitate your virtues, especially the virtues of trust, fortitude, and humility. By that love which you have for Jesus and Mary, and the love which they have for you, obtain for me the grace to live a holy life and die in their love. Amen.

For Healing from Wounds and Sins Against Purity

O Saint Joseph, most pure spouse of the Blessed Virgin and protector of the Church, grant, through your intercession, the healing of my thoughts, will, and desires.

Purify my mind of all images and memories that would turn me away from the love of God.

Purify my will from all inclinations that would tempt to choose anything less than heaven.

Purify my heart for the love of your most precious Son, who is my Way, my Truth, and my Life.

I ask this all for the glory of Christ through the Immaculate Heart of Mary, ever virgin. Amen.

For Faith That Resists Temptation

O Saint Joseph, my protector and model of every virtue, obtain for me an ardent faith which is the foundation of all holiness and my eternal union with God. Obtain for me a faith that triumphs over temptations, conquers human respect, and remains unshaken when faced with hardship and suffering. Following your example, I want to live by faith and offer my heart and my understanding to God until the day that I join you and all the angels and saints in heaven to praise and thank God for all eternity. Amen.

For Healing from Sexual Abuse

Lord, you called me into being and made me good. You graced me with your life in Baptism. Because of this, I can trust that you love me with the tenderness of a mother and the strength of a loving father. Yet things have been done to me that cause me to feel ashamed, unclean, and unworthy. Heal my memory of the wounds of abuse. Restore my self-esteem and heal my fear of intimacy and trust. Help me to build good relationships with others. Keep reminding me that you made all of me good: body and soul. Forgive those who harmed and violated me. Heal them of their disorders. May I never harm others in any way. Grant me courage to begin anew in peace, serenity, confidence, and grace. Amen.

For Modesty and Self-Discipline

Saint Joseph, chaste guardian of the Virgin Mary, to you I entrust the integrity of my body and soul. Through the help of God's grace and your intercession I hope to remain honorable in all my actions. My desire is to be pure in thought and word and embrace a deep sense of modesty that will be reflected in my external conduct.

Grant me the strength to practice self-discipline and to resist whatever could extinguish the light of grace in my soul. Safeguard my heart against the suggestions of sinful pleasures and fortify my will in my daily struggle to follow the path of virtue until the day I join the saints and angels in heaven to praise God for all eternity. Amen.

Prayer to Combat Pornography

O Saint Joseph, terror of demons and faithful protector of families, set free, by your mighty intercession, all souls held captive by the sins of pornography. By the grace of almighty God, shatter all spiritual and human bonds that separate them from the merciful love of Christ.

By your heavenly power, cast down all the works of those who would seek to use the media for the temptation and ruin of souls.

As once you protected the Holy Family from harm and peril, be our defense now against all the forces of hell and our constant guide toward the joy of heaven. Amen.

SAINT JOSEPH

PATRON OF A HAPPY DEATH

Saint Joseph is the protector and model of the dying because he prepared himself for a tranquil death throughout his life. Having loved and served Jesus and Mary all his life, he was aided by them at his death.

Blessed James Alberione

Introduction

ALTHOUGH IT MAY be difficult to accept the fact, some day we will all die. We don't know the day or the hour when God will call us home. For this reason the mystery of death can be a source of anxiety, especially as one grows older or if one suffers from a terminal or chronic illness. So it is wise to learn to put our trust in God's merciful plan for us, living in the knowledge that God will not abandon us to our fears at the moment of death.

The death of Saint Joseph is not recorded in the Gospels, but we assume it took place before that of Jesus because at the crucifixion Jesus entrusted the care of Mary to one of his disciples. According to common Church tradition, Joseph most likely died before Jesus began his public ministry. We can believe that he passed from this life with Jesus and Mary at his side to comfort him. What a beautiful image. Surely it would have been the most serene death a person could experience.

Thoughtful reflection on Saint Joseph breathing his last in the presence of Jesus and Mary can be a great source of comfort for us. We do not know when God will call us home, but while we await the time of our own death we can do our best to lead a life of integrity and goodness modeled on the life of Saint Joseph. Then when that day comes our transition from this life to eternal life will be a moment of peace, comfort, and hope. Having recourse to Saint Joseph during this life grants us assurance that Jesus, Mary, and Joseph will be at our side leading us into eternity. We can also ask Saint Joseph to intercede for a family member or a friend who might be near the point of crossing the threshold of eternal life. Pray to Saint Joseph for the grace of a happy death for yourself and your loved ones.

Prayer for a Happy Death

Saint Joseph, protector of the dying, I ask you to intercede for all the dying, and I invoke your assistance in the hour of my own death. You merited a happy passing by a holy life, and in your last hours you had the great consolation of being assisted by Jesus and Mary. Deliver me from sudden death; obtain for me the grace to imitate you in life, to detach my heart from everything worldly, and daily to gather treasures for the moment of my death. Obtain for me the grace to receive the sacrament of the sick well, and, with Mary, fill my heart with sentiments of faith, hope, love, and sorrow for sins, so that I may breathe forth my soul in peace. Amen.

Blessed James Alberione

For Deliverance from Sudden Death

O Glorious Saint Joseph, I choose you today for my patron in life and at the hour of my death. Increase in me the spirit of prayer and dedication in the service of God. Keep far from me every stain of sin; do not allow my death to come upon me unexpectedly, but grant that I may have sufficient time to confess my sins sacramentally and repent with complete understanding and sincere and perfect contrition, so that I may breathe forth my soul into the hands of Jesus and Mary. Amen.

Invocations for a Happy Death

O Blessed Joseph, you gave up your last breath in the loving embrace of Jesus and Mary. Obtain for me this grace, O holy Joseph, to breathe forth my soul in the arms of Jesus and Mary.

Jesus, Mary, and Joseph, I give you my heart and my soul.

Jesus, Mary, and Joseph, be with me at the hour of my death.

Jesus, Mary, and Joseph, may I breathe forth my soul in peace with you.

For the Grace of a Holy Death

Almighty Creator of all, I adore you
and I ask of you the grace of a holy death.
Let me die, like the glorious Saint Joseph,

in the arms of Jesus and Mary,
repeating in turn each of these sweet names
which I hope to bless throughout eternity.
Saint Joseph, obtain for me the grace
of dying the death of the just. Amen.

For the Dying

Saint Joseph, foster father of Jesus Christ, and true spouse of the Virgin Mary, pray for us and for those who will die this day/night.

Invocations for the Dying

Eternal Father, by your love for Saint Joseph whom you chose from among all men to represent your divine fatherhood here on earth, have mercy on us and on all those who will die this day.

Our Father, Hail Mary, Glory Be.

Eternal Son, by your love for Saint Joseph who was your faithful guardian on earth, have mercy on us and on all those who will die this day.

Our Father, Hail Mary, Glory Be.

Eternal Spirit, by your love for Saint Joseph who so carefully watched over Mary, your beloved spouse, have mercy on us and on all those who will die this day.

Our Father, Hail Mary, Glory Be.

For Those at the Point of Death

O Saint Joseph, protector of those in their last moments of life, take pity on those who are suffering their final battle. Take pity on my soul, too, when the hour of death shall come upon me. Do not abandon me but show that you are my good father and grant me your assistance. In your kindness intercede for me that my divine Savior may receive me with mercy into that dwelling where the elect enjoy life that shall never end. Amen.

Psalm 130—Out of the Depths

A prayer of hope in God's unfailing love and mercy not only for every individual but for the whole Church, the Israel of God.

Out of the depths I call to you, O Lord.
Lord, listen to my voice.

Let your ears be attentive
  to the voice of my supplication.
If you, O LORD, keep an account of sins,
  LORD, who could stand?
But with you there is forgiveness
  so that you may be revered.
I wait for the LORD, as does my soul,
  and I trust in his word.
My soul waits for the LORD
  more than watchmen for the dawn,
  yes, more than watchmen wait for the dawn.
O Israel, hope in the LORD,
  for with the LORD there is loving kindness,
  and bounteous redemption,
and he will redeem Israel
  from all its sins.

Glory to the Father . . .

SAINT JOSEPH

PROTECTOR OF THE
UNIVERSAL CHURCH

God trusted Joseph, as did Mary, who found in him someone who would not only save her life, but would always provide for her and her child. In this sense, Saint Joseph could not be other than the Guardian of the Church, for the Church is the continuation of the Body of Christ in history, even as Mary's motherhood is reflected in the motherhood of the Church. In his continued protection of the Church, Joseph continues to protect the child and his mother.

Pope Francis, *Patris Corde*, 5

Introduction

THE DIVINELY APPOINTED vocation of Saint Joseph did not end when he died. During his life he was the guardian and protector of Jesus and Mary, and with his death his mission expanded to include all the members of Christ's Church. Since his mission on earth was to guard and care for the physical body of Christ on earth, his mission now is to continue to care for the Mystical Body of Christ, the Church. From heaven Saint Joseph continues his role as guardian and protector of the universal Church.

Pope Pius IX declared Saint Joseph Patron of the Universal Church on December 8, 1870. It was a difficult and challenging time in the Church's history and the Pope wanted to place the Church under the powerful patronage of Joseph because Mary, his spouse, always turned to him in time of tribulation.

Saint Joseph's role as universal patron is not only to protect the Church, but to serve as a model for the whole Christian community. Whatever their stage in life, those who are devoted to Saint Joseph receive graces to overcome material and spiritual obstacles.

The prayer of Pope Leo XIII, *To You, O Blessed Joseph* (p. 145), asks the guardian of the Holy Family to defend the Church from the snares of Satan, to protect the members of the body of Christ from all spiritual dangers, and to intercede on behalf of the whole human family. Saint Joseph's heart is overflowing with love and goodness and responds with fatherly generosity to everyone who asks with confidence and right intention.

Saint Joseph, Protector of the Church

Saint Joseph, be our protector. May your interior spirit of peace, silence, good work, and prayer for the cause of Holy Church always be our inspiration. May your spirit bring us joy in union with your blessed spouse, our sweet and gentle Immaculate Mother, and in the strong yet tender love of Jesus, the glorious and immortal King of all ages and people. Amen.

Saint John XXIII

Saint Joseph, Defender of the Church

O glorious Saint Joseph, you were chosen by God to be the foster father of Jesus, the chaste spouse of Mary, ever virgin, and the head of the Holy Family; you were declared by the Vicar of Christ to be the heavenly patron and defender of the Church founded by Jesus Christ. With great confidence, therefore, I ask your powerful help for the Church on earth. With your fatherly love protect especially our Holy Father, the Pope, and all the bishops and priests united to the See of Peter. Defend all who labor for the Gospel amid the trials and hardships of this life. May all the people of the earth find a spiritual home in that Church which is the ark of salvation for all. Amen.

Saint Joseph, Patron of Canada

O Saint Joseph, we bless the Lord with you and through you.

God chose you from among all men to become the chaste spouse of Mary as she stood at the threshold of the mystery of divine maternity. Following her example, you welcomed her maternity with faith as the working of the Holy Spirit.

You became Jesus' legal father, thus making him a member of the house of David.

With constancy and affectionate concern you watched over Mother and Child to enable them to accomplish their mission. During his childhood and adolescence, Jesus, our Savior, docilely submitted himself to you as to a father. You instructed him about the details of daily living, meanwhile sharing life with him and adoring his mystery.

Continue to protect the whole Church, the family born of the salvation brought by Jesus. In particular, protect the people of Canada, who have been placed under your patronage. Help them to approach the mystery of Christ with the dispositions of faith, submission, and love that you had.

Look upon the spiritual and material needs of all who have recourse to your intercession—in particular, families and all who are poor with various forms of poverty. Through you they are sure of being led to the maternal gaze of Mary and the saving hand of Jesus.

And you, blessed Brother Andre Bessette, college doorkeeper and guardian of Saint Joseph's Oratory, open to the hopes of all who continue to seek your aid, teach them to trust in the power of prayer, as well as personal conversion and the sacramental life.

Through your intercession and that of Saint Joseph, may the Lord continue to shower graces on the Congregation of the Holy Cross, on all who visit the Oratory, on the city of Montreal, on the people of Quebec, on all the Canadian people, and on the entire Church.

Saint John Paul II
(on his visit to the shrine
of Saint Joseph in Montreal)

For the Universal Church

Saint Joseph, protector of the universal Church, look kindly upon the Pope, the bishops, the clergy, the religious and laity; pray for the sanctification of all. The Church is the fruit of the blood of Jesus, your foster Son. To you we entrust our petitions: that the Church may extend to every corner of the world; that she enjoy the freedom to teach and preach the Gospel message; that all nations acknowledge the truth of her doctrine. Defend the Church from errors, from evil and from the powers of darkness, as you once saved the threatened life of Jesus from the hands of Herod. May the desire of Jesus come true: "That there be one fold under one shepherd." Amen.

Blessed James Alberione

For the Pilgrim Church

Great Saint Joseph, placed by God
over the Holy Family at Nazareth,
be a father to the whole People of God
throughout the world
who call you their patron and protector,

shield the Holy Church of God from all harm
as it goes its pilgrim way.
Pray to God that it be kept in purity of faith,
humility of heart,
and docility to the Holy Spirit's leading,
as you yourself were in your earthly pilgrimage.
Teach it by your example
how to serve Christ in all men.
Foster in it the spirit of charity—
such love as filled it in its origins
in the Holy Family fostered by you at Nazareth.

For Persecuted Christians

O God of all the nations, the One God who is and
was and always will be, in your Providence you willed
that your Church be united to the suffering of your
Son. Look with mercy on your servants who are persecuted for their faith in you. Grant them perseverance
and courage to be worthy imitators of Christ. Bring
your wisdom upon leaders of nations to work for peace
among all peoples. May your Spirit open conversion for
those who contradict your will, that we may live in

harmony. Give us the grace to be united in truth and freedom and to always seek your will in our lives. Through Christ our Lord. Amen.

Our Lady, Queen of Peace, pray for us.

Saint Joseph, Protector of the Universal Church, pray for us.

For the Pope

O God, shepherd and ruler of all your faithful people, look with mercy upon your servant N., whom you have chosen as the chief Shepherd to preside over your Church. Grant, we pray, that you help him edify, both by word and example, those over whom he has charge, that he may attain everlasting life together with the flock entrusted to him. Through Christ our Lord. Amen.

Lord, safeguard our Holy Father, the Pope. Be his light, his strength, his consolation.

For Bishops, Priests, and Deacons

Dear Saint Joseph who carried the infant Jesus in your blessed arms and who for thirty years lived in family life with him, take under your powerful protection all bishops, priests, and deacons whom God has called as ordained ministers to continue the mission of Jesus Christ by preaching and proclaiming his Gospel, celebrating the sacraments, and shepherding the people entrusted to them.

Sustain them in their fatigue and work, strengthen them in their struggles, protect them from the evils of sin. Obtain for them the humility of John the Baptist, the faith of Saint Peter, the zeal and charity of Saint Paul, the purity of Saint John, the spirit of prayer and contemplation of which you yourself are the model, so that after striving, here on earth, to be faithful stewards of the mysteries of your foster Son, Jesus, they may in heaven receive their promised reward according to the heart of God. Amen.

For a Particular Priest

O glorious Saint Joseph, I present to you today Father *N.*, priest of Jesus Christ, and I ask you to be his advocate and defender, counselor and friend. Open your heart to him as you opened your home to the Virgin Mother. Protect his priestly vocation as you protected the life of the infant Christ when threatened by

Herod. In darkness bring him light; in weakness, strength; and in fear the peace that surpasses understanding. For the sake of the love that bound you to the Virgin Mary and to the infant Christ, be for him, O Saint Joseph, a constant intercessor and a shield against every danger of body, mind, and soul so that, in spite of his weaknesses and failings, his priesthood may bring glory to Christ and serve to increase the beauty of holiness in his bride the Church. Amen.

SAINT JOSEPH

PRAYERS, DEVOTIONS, AND PRACTICES IN HIS HONOR

Prayers

Short Prayer to Saint Joseph

Saint Joseph, if you were in my place, what would you want done for you? Please do it for me!

Saint Andre Bessette

To You, O Blessed Joseph— The October Prayer

This prayer to Saint Joseph was composed by Pope Leo XIII in the encyclical letter, Quamquam pluries, in 1889. He asked that it be prayed after the Salve Regina (Hail, Holy Queen) at the conclusion of the Rosary, especially during the month of October.

To you, O blessed Joseph, we have recourse in our tribulations, and having implored the help of your most holy spouse, we confidently invoke your patronage also. By that love which united you to the Immaculate Virgin, Mother of God, and by the fatherly affection with which you embraced the Child Jesus, we humbly pray that you look graciously on the inheritance that Jesus Christ purchased with his blood and assist us in our needs by your powerful intercession. Most watchful guardian of the Holy Family, protect the chosen people of Jesus Christ; keep far from us, most loving father, all blight of error and corruption; mercifully assist us from heaven, most mighty defender, in our struggle against the powers of darkness; and as of old you rescued the Child Jesus when in peril of his life, so now defend the Holy Church of God from the snares of the enemy and all adversity. Keep us one and all under your continual protection, in order that by your example and supported by your help, we may be enabled to lead a holy life, die a happy death, and come at last to possess eternal blessedness in heaven. Amen.

Pope Leo XIII

Unfailing Prayer to Saint Joseph

The following invocation is traditionally prayed for nine days before the feast of Saint Joseph, beginning on March 10. Dedicated devotees of Saint Joseph affirm that this prayer has never been known to fail, provided that the request is for one's spiritual benefit or that of another for whom we are praying.

O Saint Joseph, whose protection is so great, so strong, and so prompt before the throne of God, I entrust to you all my intentions and desires.

O Saint Joseph, assist with your powerful intercession, and obtain for me all spiritual blessings through your adopted Son, Jesus Christ our Lord, so that, securing here on earth your heavenly power, I offer my thanks and homage to the most loving of fathers.

O Saint Joseph, I never tire of contemplating you with Jesus asleep in your arms. I dare not approach while he rests his head near your heart. Embrace him in my name, kiss his tender face for me, and ask him to return the kiss when I draw my last breath.

Saint Joseph, patron of departed souls, pray for me (*mention your request*). Amen.

Thirty Days' Prayer to Saint Joseph

This prayer honors Saint Joseph for each of the thirty years he spent with Jesus and Mary here on earth. While it can be recited during any thirty-day period, it is fitting to invoke his intercession during the time preceding his feast on March 19.

Ever blessed and glorious Joseph, kind and loving father, and helpful friend of all in sorrow! You are the good father and protector of orphans, the defender of the defenseless, the patron of those in need. Look kindly on my request. My sins have displeased God, and for this I am filled with unhappiness. Loving guardian of the Family of Nazareth, I turn to you for help and protection.

Listen, I beg you, with fatherly concern, to my earnest prayers, and obtain for me the favor I ask.

I ask it by the infinite mercy of the eternal Son of God, which moved him to take on our nature and to be born into this world.

I ask it by the fatigue and suffering you endured when you found no shelter at the inn in Bethlehem for the holy Virgin, nor a lodging where the Son of God could be born. Then, being everywhere refused, you had to allow the Queen of Heaven to give birth to the world's Redeemer in a cave.

I ask it by the beauty and power of that sacred name, Jesus, which you conferred on the loveable infant.

I ask it by that anguish you felt at the prophecy of holy Simeon, who declared that the Child Jesus and his holy Mother would be victims of our sins and of their great love for us.

I ask it through your distress and sadness of soul when the angel declared to you that the life of the Child Jesus was sought by his enemies. Due to their evil plan you had to flee with him and his Blessed Mother to Egypt. I ask it by all the suffering, weariness, and labors of that long and dangerous journey.

I ask it by all your care to protect the Sacred Child and his Immaculate Mother during your second journey, when you were told by the angel to return to your own country. I ask it by your peaceful life in Nazareth where you experienced so many joys and sorrows.

I ask it by your great distress when Jesus was lost to you and his Mother for three days. I ask it by your joy at finding him in the Temple, and by the comfort you found at Nazareth while living in the company of Jesus. I ask it by the love and respect he showed in his obedience to you.

I ask it by the perfect love and conformity you showed in accepting the divine will to depart from this life and from the company of Jesus and Mary. I ask it by the joy that filled your soul when the Redeemer of the world, triumphant over death and hell, entered into the possession of his kingdom, led you into heaven, and bestowed on you special honors.

I ask it through Mary's glorious Assumption, and through that endless happiness you have with her in the presence of God.

O good father! I beg you, by all your sufferings, sorrows, and joys, to hear me and obtain for me what I ask (*make your request*).

Obtain for all those who have asked my prayers everything that is useful to them in the plan of God. Finally, my dear patron and father, be with me and all who are dear to me in our last moments, that we may eternally sing the praises of Jesus, Mary, and Joseph. Amen.

Akathist Hymn to Saint Joseph

Akathist *hymns come from the Eastern Christian tradition. (Akathist comes from the Greek word meaning "not seated;" the participants stand as they sing.) They are sung in honor of one of the Persons of the Trinity, the Blessed Virgin Mary, another saint, or an event in the life of Jesus or Mary. The following is a short excerpt from the* Akathist *Hymn to Saint Joseph, the Betrothed.*

Having heard in the Scriptures of the Lord who said: Behold, a virgin shall conceive and bear a son, Emmanuel, you did believe what was told to you by the angel, O righteous Joseph; and like a sealed book, wherein the Word was inscribed by the finger of the Father, you took Mary into your own house, and like a servant you waited upon her with fear and zeal. Therefore, we cry to you:

Rejoice! For you set your heart to understand the law of God!

Rejoice! For you opened your mind to receive the mysteries of God!

Rejoice! For before all men you were vouchsafed

to know the great mystery of piety that God
has appeared upon earth!

Rejoice! For you perceived his coming to be for
the salvation of men from their sins!

Rejoice! For without doubting you believed what
was revealed to you!

Rejoice! For your faith was accounted onto you as
righteousness!

Rejoice! O righteous Joseph, ready helper and
intercessor for our souls!

Taking the divinely chosen maiden into your home,
O blessed Joseph, you loved her as your betrothed, you
honored her as the most-holy Virgin and Mother of
the Savior of the world, and you ministered to her with
fear and reverence, striving with all your soul to keep all
that was written in the Law and the Prophets; and with
Mary you cried out to God: ALLELUIA!

Beholding in the manger of Bethlehem the Star
that shone forth from Jacob, you first worshipped the
newborn; and when heaven offered him a star, the
angels hymnody, the shepherds testimony, and the
Magi worship and gifts, you, O righteous Joseph,

offered your whole self as a gift to the Lord, dedicating your life, cares, and labors to his service. Therefore, we cry to you:

Rejoice! You who before all others beheld the descent to earth of the unsetting Sun of Righteousness!

Rejoice! First witness and servant on earth of the incarnate Son of God, who was born of the Father before all ages!

Rejoice! Earthly carpenter who was vouchsafed to be called the father of the heavenly Architect!

Rejoice! Protector and guardian of the Infant to whom the ranks of angels minister with fear!

Rejoice! Reverent servant of the Mother of God, the Word!

Rejoice! O righteous Joseph, ready helper and intercessor for our souls!

Prayer of Trust in the Goodness of Saint Joseph

The following is a prayer, recommended by Pope Francis, from a nineteenth-century French prayer book of the Congregation of the Sisters of Jesus and Mary.

Glorious Patriarch Saint Joseph, whose power makes the impossible possible, come to my aid in these times of anguish and difficulty. Take under your protection the serious and troubling situations that I commend to you, that they may have a happy outcome. My beloved father, all my trust is in you. Let it not be said that I invoked you in vain, and since you can do everything with Jesus and Mary, show me that your goodness is as great as your power. Amen.

Short Novena to Saint Joseph

O Glorious Saint Joseph, steadfast follower of Jesus Christ, I am confident that your prayers for me will be graciously heard at the throne of God.

To you I lift my heart and hands asking your powerful intercession to obtain from the compassionate Heart of Jesus all the graces necessary for my spiritual and temporal well-being, particularly the grace of a happy death, and the special grace for which I now pray (*mention your request*).

Pray the following seven times in honor of the seven joys and seven sorrows of Saint Joseph:

℣. Saint Joseph, guardian of the Word Incarnate, by the love you bear for Jesus Christ, and for the glory of his name.

℟. Hear my prayer and obtain my petitions.

Memorare to Saint Joseph

Remember, O most chaste spouse of the Virgin Mary, that never was it known that anyone who asked for your help or sought your intercession was left unaided. Inspired by this confidence, I commend myself to you and beg your protection. Despise not my petition, dear foster father of our Redeemer, but hear and answer my prayer. Amen.

Prayer to the Sleeping Saint Joseph

(A devotion made popular by Pope Francis)

"I have great love for Saint Joseph, because he is a man of silence and strength. On my table I have an image of Saint Joseph sleeping. Even when he is asleep, he is taking care of the Church! When I have a problem, a difficulty, I write a little note and I put it underneath Saint Joseph, so that he can dream about it! In other words I tell him: pray for this problem!

"Joseph's rest revealed God's will to him. In this moment of rest in the Lord, as we pause from our many daily obligations and activities, God is also speaking to us. . . . But like Saint Joseph, once we have heard God's voice, we must rise from our slumber; we must get up and act."

Pope Francis in an address to families, 2015

O Saint Joseph, you are a man greatly favored by the Most High. The angel of the Lord appeared to you in dreams, while you slept, to warn you and guide you as you cared for the Holy Family. You were both silent and strong, a loyal and courageous protector.

Dear Saint Joseph, as you rest in the Lord, confident of his absolute power and goodness, look upon me. Please take my need into your heart, dream of it, and present it to Jesus (*mention your request*).

Help me then, good Saint Joseph, to hear the voice of God, to arise, and to act with love. I praise and thank God with joy.

Saint Joseph, I love you. Amen.

Hail, Guardian of the Redeemer

Hail, Guardian of the Redeemer,
spouse of the Blessed Virgin Mary.
To you God entrusted his only Son;
in you Mary placed her trust;
with you Christ became man.
Blessed Joseph, to us too,
show yourself a father
and guide us in the path of life.
Obtain for us grace, mercy, and courage,
and defend us from every evil. Amen.

Pope Francis

Prayer of Praise and Thanksgiving

It is a good spiritual practice to praise and thank God for the graces and privileges bestowed upon the saints.

Lord Jesus, I praise, glorify, and bless you for all the graces and privileges you have bestowed upon Joseph, your foster father and servant. By his merits grant me your grace, and through his intercession help me in all my needs. At the hour of my death be with me until that time when I can join the saints in heaven to praise you forever and ever.

Devotions

Seven Sundays in Honor of the
Seven Sorrows and Seven Joys of Saint Joseph

DEVOTION OF THE Seven Sundays to honor the seven sorrows and seven joys of Saint Joseph may be practiced at any time of the year. Devotees of Saint Joseph have followed the custom to venerate him especially on the seven Sundays preceding his feast.

It is recommended that on each Sunday one attends Mass and receives Holy Communion in honor of Saint Joseph, that time be set aside to contemplate the Scripture passages commemorating his seven sorrows and seven joys, and that the prayers be recited in a spirit of praise and confidence.

These prayers can also be prayed all at once whenever one would like to meditate on the sorrows and joys of Saint Joseph.

FIRST SUNDAY

When his mother Mary was betrothed to Joseph, but before they came together, she was found to be with child by the Holy Spirit. Joseph her husband was a good and upright man so he was planning to put her away, but quietly because he did not wish to disgrace her. But while he was thinking these things over, behold, an angel of the Lord appeared to him in a dream and said, "Joseph son of David, do not be afraid to take your wife Mary into your house—the child who has been conceived in her is from the Holy Spirit. She will give birth to a son and you shall name him Jesus, because he will save his people from their sins."

Mt 1:18–22

Saint Joseph, what anguish must have filled your heart when you thought of ending your betrothal to Mary, and "put her away" quietly to not disgrace her. And what profound joy you must have experienced when the mystery of the incarnation was revealed to you.

By this sorrow and joy of yours, I ask that you walk with me through the uncertainties in my life. Teach me how to surrender to the Lord the moments of confusion, to listen with my heart when the Spirit speaks to me so that, like you, I may accomplish all that the Lord has planned for me.

Our Father, Hail Mary, Glory Be.

Second Sunday

Since Joseph was of the house and family of David he went up from Nazareth in Galilee to Bethlehem of Judea, the city of David, to be registered with Mary, who was betrothed to him and who was pregnant. It happened that while they were there the day came for her to give birth. She gave birth to her firstborn son, wrapped him swaddling clothes, and laid him in a manger, because there was no room for them in the inn.

Lk 2:4–7

Saint Joseph, while chosen by God to be the foster father of the Word made flesh, you still suffered distress at having to accept the shelter of a stable for Mary to give birth. But the deprivation you experienced must have turned to joy when you heard angels heralding the birth of the Savior.

By this sorrow and joy of yours, I ask you to intercede before the Lord for those who are without food and shelter for themselves and their families. Ask our heavenly Father to open the hearts of the leaders of nations to understand and acknowledge the dignity of the human person so that the necessities of life are provided for all God's children.

Our Father, Hail Mary, Glory Be.

And when eight days had passed for his circumcision they gave him the name Jesus, the name given him by the angel before he was conceived in the womb.

Lk 2:21

Saint Joseph, even while you faithfully obeyed the Law, surely you were saddened at the sight of the blood shed by the infant Savior at his circumcision. At the same time the name "Jesus" must have filled you with new hope and profound joy.

By this sorrow and joy of yours, teach me to value the laws of God and the Church, and to always speak the name of Jesus with reverence. Ask our heavenly Father to bless all children; may God grant them a vibrant faith to sustain them, an abiding hope to encourage them, and a steadfast love for Jesus to accompany them along life's way.

Our Father, Hail Mary, Glory Be.

His father and mother were amazed at what was said about Jesus. And Simeon blessed them and said to his mother, Mary, "Behold, he is destined to bring about the fall and rise of many in Israel, and to be a sign that will be opposed (And a sword will pierce your own soul) so that the thoughts of many hearts may be revealed."

Lk 2:33–35

Saint Joseph, the words of Simeon must have gripped your heart with foreboding and perhaps even a sense of powerlessness to prevent the suffering that Mary must have endured when she heard the prophecy. Yet what joy you must have felt knowing that the salvation foretold by Simeon would be offered to all peoples.

By this sorrow and joy of yours, ask the Lord to grant me a deeper trust in the promises God has made, so that I may proclaim the message of salvation through my words and actions.

Our Father, Hail Mary, Glory Be.

Fifth Sunday

An angel of the Lord appeared to Joseph in a dream and said, "Get up, take the child and his mother, and flee to Egypt, and remain there until I tell you; Herod is about to search for the child to destroy him." Then Joseph got up, took the child and his mother by night, and went to Egypt, and remained there until the death of Herod.

Mt 2:13–15, NRSV

Saint Joseph, watchful guardian of the incarnate Son of God, you listened to the Spirit's inspiration to flee to Egypt though it meant hardship and struggle. Still, because you were a caring parent and devoted spouse, surely you rejoiced to have been able to protect and provide for Jesus and Mary in an unfamiliar, hostile land.

By this sorrow and joy of yours, obtain for me the grace to always listen to the voice of my conscience urging me to follow after those things that will lead to eternal happiness. Intercede before the Lord for all those who are forced to live in a strange land, those who are poor and in need, and those who are without a home or employment. In their time of hardship be their protector and provider.

Our Father, Hail Mary, Glory Be.

Sixth Sunday

When Herod died, an angel of the Lord suddenly appeared in a dream to Joseph in Egypt and said, "Get up, take the child and his mother, and go to the land of Israel, for those who were seeking the child's life are dead." Then Joseph got up, took the child and his mother, and went to the land of Israel.

Mt 2:19–21, NRSV

They returned to Galilee to their own city, Nazareth. The child grew and became strong and was filled with wisdom, and the grace of God was on him.

Lk 2:39–40

Saint Joseph, your consolation in having brought Jesus and Mary safely out of the land of Egypt must have been burdened at times by the fear that Herod's successor would also seek out the child to kill him. But despite your fear, you set about to live an ordinary and happy life at Nazareth in the company of Jesus and Mary, placing your trust in the Lord.

By this sorrow and joy of yours, obtain for me the grace of an abiding confidence in God. In difficult circumstances teach me how to recognize the Lord's will for myself and my family, so that all that I do, although hidden or simple, may reflect your love.

Our Father, Hail Mary, Glory Be.

And it happened that after three days they found him in the Temple, seated in the midst of the teachers. . . . When his parents saw him they were amazed and his mother said to him, "Son, why did you do this to us? You see your father and I have been looking for you, worried to death!" And he said to them, "Why were you looking for me? Did you not know that I have to concern myself with my Father's affairs?" And they did not understand what he was telling them. Then he went down with them and went to Nazareth, and he was subject to them. His mother kept all these things in her heart.

Lk 2:46–52

Saint Joseph, when the child Jesus was lost for three days, you must have been plagued by worry while you sought him. Then, how happy you must have been when you and Mary found him in the Temple, sitting in the midst of the teachers, listening to them and asking them questions.

By this sorrow and joy of yours, ask the Lord to bless each member of my family and keep them safe from harm. Intercede before God for the family of nations so that discord may give way to harmony, hostility to forgiveness, rivalry to acceptance.

Our Father, Hail Mary, Glory Be.

Devotion of the First Wednesday of the Month

The first Wednesday of the month is dedicated to Saint Joseph for these intentions: that he will protect the universal Church; that he will help us in time of need; that he will assist and console the dying; that he will provide for all of our spiritual and material needs.

English:

Behold the faithful and prudent servant whom the Lord God has set over his household.

Latin:

Ecce fidélis servus et prudens queur constituit Dóminus super famíliam suam.

O Saint Joseph, faithful cooperator in our redemption, have pity on poor humanity, still wrapped in so much error and so many evils. You were a docile instrument in the hands of the heavenly Father, in arranging everything for the birth and childhood of Jesus, for the preparation of the Victim, of the Priest, and of the Divine Master of the world. Saint most docile to the will of God, obtain for us zeal for vocations and for their formation. For ourselves, we ask you for generous and constant correspondence to the precious gift of God's call.

Saint Joseph, pray for us.

O Saint Joseph, model of every virtue, obtain for us your interior spirit. In loving and active silence, in the practice of all religious and civil laws, in docility to everything God willed, you arrived at a high degree of sanctity and heavenly glory. Obtain for us an increase of faith, hope, and charity, an ample infusion of the cardinal virtues, and an abundance of the gifts of the Holy Spirit.

Saint Joseph, pray for us.

O Saint Joseph, we venerate you as the model of laborers, the friend of the poor, the consoler of the afflicted and those forced to leave their own land, the saint of Divine Providence. On earth you represented the universal goodness and concern of the heavenly Father. You were the carpenter of Nazareth and work-teacher to the Son of God, who became a humble laborer for us. Assist with your prayers all who labor in intellectual, moral, and physical work. For the nations obtain legislation inspired by the Gospel, the spirit of

Christian charity, a way of governing in accord with justice and peace.

Saint Joseph, pray for us.

O Saint Joseph, foster father of Jesus, we bless the Lord for your intimate communication with him during his infancy and youth at Bethlehem, in Egypt, and at Nazareth. You loved him with a father's love, and he loved you with the love of a son. Your faith made you adore in him the incarnate Son of God, while he obeyed you, served you, listened to you. You held pleasant conversations with him; shared work, great sufferings, and most tender consolations. Obtain for us the grace never to offend Jesus by sin. Pray for us that we may always receive the sacraments of Holy Eucharist and Reconciliation well, attain to a great intimacy with and a tender and strong love for Jesus while on earth, and possess him forever in heaven.

Saint Joseph, pray for us.

O Saint Joseph, pure spouse of Mary, we humbly ask you to obtain for us a true devotion to our tender Mother, Teacher, and Queen. By divine will, your mission was associated with Mary's. With Mary you shared sufferings and joys; with her there was a holy rivalry in virtue, work, and merits; union of mind and of heart. Saint Joseph, pray for fathers and mothers. Obtain for us the grace to know the Blessed Virgin Mary, to imitate her, to love her, to pray to her always. Draw many souls to her maternal heart.

Saint Joseph, pray for us.

O Saint Joseph, protector of the dying, we supplicate you for all the dying and beg your assistance in the hour of our own death. You merited a happy passing by a holy life, and in your last hours you had the ineffable consolation of being assisted by Jesus and Mary. Deliver us from sudden death; obtain for us the grace to imitate you in life, to detach our heart from everything worldly, and daily to gather treasures for the moment of our death. Obtain for us the grace to receive the sacraments of the sick well, and, with Mary, inspire us with sentiments of faith, hope, love, and sorrow for sins, so that we may breathe forth our soul in peace.

Saint Joseph, pray for us.

O Saint Joseph, protector of the universal Church, look kindly upon the Pope, the episcopate, the clergy, the religious, and the laity. Pray for the sanctification of all. The Church is the fruit of the blood of Jesus, your foster Son. We entrust to you our supplications for the extension, liberty, and exaltation of the Church. Defend her from errors, from evil, and from the powers of hell, as you once saved the threatened life of Jesus from the hands of Herod. May the desire of Jesus come true: "That there be one fold under one shepherd."

Saint Joseph, pray for us.

Blessed James Alberione

The Rosary in Honor of Saint Joseph

THE ROSARY IS a blend of contemplative and vocal prayer. While reciting the familiar prayers, we can reflect and meditate on the individual mysteries. Praying the Rosary is a spiritual help to grow in virtue and deepen our prayer life.

The Rosary of Saint Joseph is an invitation to pray with the Blessed Mother, contemplate the life of the Holy Family, and ponder the virtues of Saint Joseph. The Rosary of Saint Joseph can be prayed using the traditional five-decade rosary and the usual prayers of the

Rosary, but with the following special list of mysteries. It is particularly effective to pray the Rosary nine days in a row as a novena. An optional way of praying this Rosary is given at the end of the mysteries.

First Mystery
Betrothal to Mary

Now the birth of Jesus came about in the following manner. When his mother Mary was betrothed to Joseph, but before they came together, she was found to be with child by the Holy Spirit.

Mt 1:18

After Jesus, no one loved Mary more than Joseph, because no one else knew her as he did, and no one was united to her with closer and stronger bonds. Saint Joseph will not fail to inspire in us the same love that he had for Mary.

Blessed James Alberione

Grace to Ask: That I may serve God in caring for those God has given me to cherish.

Our Father, ten Hail Marys, Glory to the Father . . .

Invocation: Saint Joseph, spouse of the Virgin Mary, teach me to imitate Mary and to love her with all my heart.

SECOND MYSTERY

The Annunciation to Joseph

Joseph her husband was a good and upright man so he was planning to put her away, but quietly because he did not wish to disgrace her. But while he was thinking these things over, behold an angel of the Lord appeared to him in a dream and said, "Joseph son of David, do not be afraid to take your wife Mary into your house—the child who has been conceived in her is from the Holy Spirit."

Mt 1:19–21

Saint Joseph lived in silent agony until he received a revelation from an angel. He could have given way to regrets and harbored excuses, but as soon as the will of God became clear, he welcomed it wholeheartedly. When we truly let God work in us and through us, as Saint Joseph did, we are set on the path to holiness.

Blessed James Alberione

Grace to Ask: That I may open my heart to greater trust in God's plan for my life.

Our Father, ten Hail Marys, Glory to the Father . . .

Invocation: Saint Joseph, silently waiting, teach me to be attentive and patient so that I might recognize God's will and act on it.

THIRD MYSTERY
The Birth and Naming of Jesus

All this took place to fulfill what was declared by the Lord through the prophet when he said,

> Behold, the virgin shall be with child and will give birth to a son,
> And they shall give him the name Emmanuel,

which is translated, "God with us." When Joseph rose from his sleep he did as the angel of the Lord had commanded him and took his wife into his house, but he had not known her before she gave birth to her son, and he gave him the name Jesus.

Mt 1:22–25

In Saint Joseph, God truly found a faithful servant whose eyes were ever turned toward him, to learn

God's desire and will and to carry them out promptly, docilely, and lovingly.

Blessed James Alberione

Grace to Ask: That I may see the hand of God at work in the events and circumstances of my life.

Our Father, ten Hail Marys, Glory to the Father . . .

Invocation: Saint Joseph, the Father's faithful servant, teach me to serve God with all my heart.

Fourth Mystery
The Flight into Egypt

After [the Wise Men] had left, an angel of the Lord appeared to Joseph in a dream and said, "Get up, take the child and his mother, and flee to Egypt, and remain there until I tell you; Herod is about to search for the child to destroy him." Then Joseph got up, took the child and his mother by night, and went to Egypt, and remained there until the death of Herod.

Mt 2:13–15, NRSV

Because of the reason and circumstances of the sudden flight into Egypt, this was one of the most difficult and heartbreaking trials of Saint Joseph. Trusting in God, he disregarded his fears and doubts and allowed himself to be guided by faith. Sustained by his love for Jesus and Mary and encouraged by the hope that God would deliver them, he overcame the dangers and hardships stemming from seemingly insurmountable difficulties.

Blessed James Alberione

Grace to Ask: That I may recognize and respond to the needs of the poor, the homeless, and the marginalized.

Our Father, ten Hail Marys, Glory to the Father . . .

Invocation: Saint Joseph, look with compassion upon the fearful, the exiled, and the homeless.

FIFTH MYSTERY
The Hidden Life at Nazareth

So having been warned in a dream, [Joseph] departed for the district of Galilee, and he went and settled in a town called Nazareth to fulfill what was said by the prophets, "he shall be called a Nazorean."

Mt 2:23

Then [Jesus] went down with them and went to Nazareth, and he was subject to them. His mother kept all these things in her heart and Jesus progressed in wisdom and age and grace before God and men.

Lk 2:51–52

Imagine the love and familiarity there must have been between Joseph and Jesus during the Savior's infancy, childhood, and adolescence. Imagine the conversations that the best father and the best son must have had together, as Saint Joseph taught Jesus the art of carpentry, instructed him in the ways of prayer, and shared the joys and sufferings of daily life.

Blessed James Alberione

Grace to Ask: That I may nurture unity and harmony in my family.

Our Father, ten Hail Marys, Glory to the Father . . .

Invocation: Saint Joseph, teach me how to live a holy life that I may die a holy death.

At the conclusion of the Rosary, you may pray the Litany of Saint Joseph (p. 184) and To You O Blessed Joseph (p. 145).

The Oblates of Saint Joseph also pray a Rosary of Saint Joseph using these mysteries but replacing the Hail Mary with the following prayer:

Joseph, son of David and husband of Mary, we honor you, Guardian of the Redeemer, and we adore the child you named Jesus. Saint Joseph, patron of the universal Church, pray for us that, like you, we may live totally dedicated to the interests of the Savior. Amen.

Chaplet of Saint Joseph

The chaplet of Saint Joseph is made up of fifteen sets of three beads (often purple in color), separated by individual beads (often white in color). On the white beads one of the Joyful, Sorrowful, and Glorious mysteries is considered and the Hail Mary is prayed. On each of the purple beads, this prayer is prayed:

Praised and blessed be Jesus, Mary, and Joseph.

The chaplet ends with the following prayer:

℣. Pray for us, O holy Saint Joseph!

℟. That we may be made worthy of the promises of Christ!

Let us pray.

O God, who prepared Saint Joseph from all eternity for the service of your eternal Son and his Blessed Mother, and made him worthy to be the spouse of this Blessed Virgin and the foster father of your Son: we beseech you, through all the services he rendered to Jesus and Mary on earth, that you would make us worthy of his intercession and grant us to enjoy the happiness of his company in heaven. Through Christ our Lord. Amen.

Litany of Saint Joseph

Lord, *have mercy on us.*

Christ, *have mercy on us.*

Lord, *have mercy on us.*

Christ, *hear us.*

Christ, *graciously hear us.*

God, the Father of heaven, *have mercy on us.*

God the Son, Redeemer of the world, *have mercy on us.*

God the Holy Spirit, *have mercy on us.*

Holy Trinity, one God, *have mercy on us.*

Holy Mary, *pray for us.*

Saint Joseph,	*pray for us.*
Esteemed offspring of David,	*pray for us.*
Light of patriarchs,	*pray for us.*
Faithful spouse of the Mother of God,	*pray for us.*
Foster father of the Son of God,	*pray for us.*
Guardian of the Holy Family,	*pray for us.*
Joseph most just,	*pray for us.*
Joseph most chaste,	*pray for us.*
Joseph most prudent,	*pray for us.*
Joseph most strong,	*pray for us.*
Joseph most obedient,	*pray for us.*
Joseph most faithful,	*pray for us.*
Mirror of patience,	*pray for us.*
Lover of poverty,	*pray for us.*
Model of workers,	*pray for us.*
Glory of home life,	*pray for us.*
Guardian of virgins,	*pray for us.*
Mainstay of families,	*pray for us.*

Hope of the sick and suffering,	*pray for us.*
Consoler of the dying,	*pray for us.*
Terror of demons,	*pray for us.*
Protector of the universal Church,	*pray for us.*

Lamb of God, you take away the sins of the world,
  spare us, O Lord.

Lamb of God, you take away the sins of the world,
  graciously hear us, O Lord.

Lamb of God, you take away the sins of the world,
  have mercy on us.

℣. The Lord made him guardian of his household,

℟. His faithful and prudent servant.

Let us pray.

O God, in your Providence you chose blessed Joseph to be the spouse of your most holy Mother. Grant that we may be worthy of the intercession of him whom we honor as our protector. We ask this through Christ, your Son. Amen.

A Triduo to Saint Joseph

This three-day devotional, written by Saint John Henry Newman, offers devotees of Saint Joseph an opportunity to meditate on the privileges and titles of a "man of eminent sanctity."

First Day

Consider the Glorious Titles of Saint Joseph.

He was the true and worthy spouse of Mary, supplying in a visible manner the place of Mary's invisible Spouse, the Holy Spirit. He was a virgin, and his virginity was the faithful mirror of the virginity of Mary. He was the cherub, placed to guard the new terrestrial paradise from the intrusion of every foe.

℣. Blessed be the name of Joseph.

℟. Henceforth and forever. Amen.

Let us pray:

O God, who in your ineffable Providence chose Blessed Joseph to be the husband of your most holy Mother, grant, we beseech you, that we may be made worthy to receive him for our intercessor in heaven, whom on earth we venerate as our holy protector; you who live and reign world without end. Amen.

Second Day
Consider the Glorious Titles of Saint Joseph.

His was the title of father of the Son of God, because he was the spouse of Mary, ever virgin. He was our Lord's father, because Jesus yielded to him the obedience of a son. He was our Lord's father, because to him were entrusted, and by him were faithfully fulfilled, the duties of a father, in protecting him, giving him a home, sustaining and rearing him, and providing him with a trade.

℣. Blessed be the name of Joseph.

℟. Henceforth and forever. Amen.

Let us pray:

O God, who in your ineffable Providence chose Blessed Joseph to be the husband of your most holy Mother, grant, we beseech you, that we may be made worthy to receive him for our intercessor in heaven, whom on earth we venerate as our holy protector; you who live and reign world without end. Amen.

Third Day

Consider the Glorious Titles of Saint Joseph.

He is Holy Joseph, because according to the opinion of a great number of Church doctors, he, as well as Saint John Baptist, was sanctified even before he was born. He is Holy Joseph, because his office, of being spouse and protector of Mary, specially demanded sanctity. He is Holy Joseph, because no other saint but he lived in such and so long an intimacy and familiarity with the source of all holiness, Jesus, God incarnate, and Mary, the holiest of creatures.

℣. Blessed be the name of Joseph.

℟. Henceforth and forever. Amen.

Let us pray:

O God, who in your ineffable Providence chose Blessed Joseph to be the husband of your most holy Mother, grant, we beseech you, that we may be made worthy to receive him for our intercessor in heaven, whom on earth we venerate as our holy protector; you who live and reign world without end. Amen.

Scriptural Novena in Honor of Saint Joseph

GENERALLY A NOVENA is made on nine consecutive days, often in preparation for a feast day, or for some particular intention. This scriptural novena can also be prayed over a nine-week period on Wednesday, which is the day traditionally associated with devotions to Saint Joseph.

After praying the psalm of the day and reading the Scripture passage, take a few moments to think about them and then offer a prayer that arises from your heart and is the fruit of your reflection. During this prayer, or when you pray the Intercessions, you may want to recall the personal intention of your novena.

DAY ONE

Invocation

(While making the Sign of the Cross)

> O Lord, open my lips,
> And my tongue will proclaim your praise.
> Glory be to the Father, and to the Son, and to the

Holy Spirit,
as it was in the beginning, is now, and will be
forever. Amen.

Antiphon

The Lord made him master of his house, and ruler
over his possessions.

Psalm 1

Happiness

Happy is the one who does not follow
the counsel of the wicked,
or persist in the ways of sinners,
or sit in the assembly of the mockers,
but instead takes delight in the law of the Lord,
and so recites from his Law day and night.
Like a tree planted by streams of water,
whose fruit comes in proper season
and whose leaves do not wither—
For the Lord concerns himself
with the way of the righteous . . ."

Glory be . . .

Antiphon

The Lord made him master of his house, and ruler over his possessions.

Reading

Mt 1:20–21, 23

Behold, an angel of the Lord appeared to him in a dream and said, "Joseph son of David, do not be afraid to take your wife Mary into your house—the child who has been conceived in her is from the Holy Spirit. She will give birth to a son and you shall name him Jesus, because he will save his people from their sins." When Joseph rose from his sleep he did as the angel of the Lord had commended him.

Reflection and spontaneous prayer of mind and heart.

Intercessions

Joseph, so prompt to obey the will of God, grant me the grace of ready obedience to the will of God relating to the circumstances of my life.

Joseph, to whom God's saving plan was revealed, teach me to know my Savior, Jesus Christ, and to love and honor his Holy Name.

Joseph, husband of the Virgin Mary, teach me to read the heart of Mary, to imitate her, and to love her with all my heart.

℣. Pray for us, Saint Joseph,

℟. That we may be made worthy of the promises of Christ.

Closing Prayer

O Lord, assisted by the prayers of the husband of your most holy Mother, grant that what we cannot obtain of ourselves, we may, through his intercession, be given by you who live and reign with the Father in the unity of the Holy Spirit, God for ever and ever. Amen.

May the divine assistance remain always with us.

And may the souls of the faithful departed through the mercy of God rest in peace. Amen.

Conclude with the Sign of the Cross.

Day Two

Invocation

O Lord, open my lips,
And my tongue will proclaim your praise.
Glory be to the Father, and to the Son, and to the
Holy Spirit,
as it was in the beginning, is now, and will be
forever. Amen.

Antiphon

Joseph was the husband of Mary, of whom was born
Jesus, the Christ.

Psalm 15

Question and Answer

O Lord, who shall abide in your tent?
Who shall dwell on your holy mountain?
The one who lives uprightly,
who practices virtue,
and is truthful to himself.
He does not go about spreading slander,
does no evil to his friend,

nor does he bring up anything
    to discredit his neighbor.
In his eyes a contemptible person is held in
        disdain,
    whereas he holds in honor those who fear the
        LORD.
    He stands by an oath although unfavorable to
        him, without changing it.
He does not lend his money on interest,
    nor does he accept a bribe against an innocent
        person.
    He who does these things will never be moved.

Glory be . . .

Antiphon

Joseph was the husband of Mary, of whom was born Jesus, the Christ.

Reading

Mt 1:18–20

Now the birth of Jesus Christ came about in the following manner. When his mother Mary was betrothed to Joseph, but before they came together, she was found to be with child by the Holy Spirit. Joseph her husband was a good and upright man so he was planning to put her away, but quietly because he did not wish to disgrace her. But while he was thinking these things over, behold an angel of the Lord appeared to him in a dream and said, "Joseph son of David do not be afraid to take your wife Mary into your house—the child who has been conceived in her is from the Holy Spirit."

Reflection and spontaneous prayer of mind and heart.

Intercessions

Joseph, so prudent even in doubt, obtain for me the grace that will free me from hasty decisions and ill-considered action.

Joseph, even in time of trial you were more concerned for Mary than for yourself; teach me how to put my own interests aside and be more concerned for others.

Joseph, silently waiting on the will of God, teach me to be still and to seek only to do the will of God.

℣. Pray for us, Saint Joseph,

℟. That we may be made worthy of the promises of Christ.

Closing Prayer

O Lord, assisted by the prayers of the husband of your most holy Mother, grant that what we cannot obtain of ourselves, we may, through his intercession, be given by you who live and reign with the Father in the unity of the Holy Spirit, God for ever and ever. Amen.

May the divine assistance remain always with us.
And may the souls of the faithful departed through the mercy of God rest in peace. Amen.

Conclude with the Sign of the Cross.

DAY THREE

Invocation

O Lord, open my lips,
And my tongue will proclaim your praise.
Glory be to the Father, and to the Son, and to the
    Holy Spirit,
as it was in the beginning, is now, and will be
    forever. Amen.

Antiphon

The faithful man will be greatly praised; and the guardian of his Lord will be glorified.

Psalm 91

Refuge and Strength

You who dwell in the shelter of the Most High
    and live in the shadow of the Almighty.
Say to the LORD: "My refuge and my fortress,
    my God in whom I trust!"
He covers you with his pinions
    and you take shelter under his wings:
    his faithfulness is a rampart and shield.
For he will command his angels concerning you,
    to guard you in all your ways:
they will carry you with their hands,
    lest you should dash your foot against a stone.
Glory be . . .

Antiphon

The faithful man will be greatly praised; and the guardian of his Lord will be glorified.

Reading

Lk 2:4–8

Since Joseph was of the house and family of David, he went up from Nazareth in Galilee to Bethlehem of Judea, the city of David, to be registered with Mary, who was betrothed to him and who was pregnant. It happened that while they were there the day came for her to give birth. She gave birth to her firstborn son, wrapped him in swaddling clothes, and laid him in a manger, because there was no room for them in the inn.

Reflection and spontaneous prayer of mind and heart.

Intercessions

Joseph, first among all men to look on the face of God-made-man, obtain for me the grace to see the face of Christ in every person I meet.

Joseph, uncomplaining on your own or Mary's account, teach me wholehearted acceptance of the will of God in my own and others' regard.

Joseph, man of silent prayer, as you carried Christ in your arms, teach me to hold him in my heart.

℣. Pray for us, Saint Joseph,

℟. That we may be made worthy of the promises of Christ.

Closing Prayer

O Lord, assisted by the prayers of the husband of your most holy Mother, grant that what we cannot obtain of ourselves, we may, through his intercession, be given by you who live and reign with the Father in the unity of the Holy Spirit, God for ever and ever. Amen.

May the divine assistance remain always with us.

And may the souls of the faithful departed through the mercy of God rest in peace. Amen.

Conclude with the Sign of the Cross.

DAY FOUR

Invocation

O Lord, open my lips,

And my tongue will proclaim your praise.

Glory be to the Father, and to the Son, and to the Holy Spirit,

as it was in the beginning, is now, and will be forever. Amen.

Antiphon

The Lord was with Joseph and guided him in all he did.

Psalm 113

The Gentleness of God

Praise, you servants of the LORD,
     Praise the name of the LORD.
May the name of the LORD be blessed
     both now, and forevermore.
The name of the LORD is to be praised
     from the rising of the sun to its setting.
The LORD is supreme over all the nations,
     his splendor is above the heavens.
Who is like the LORD our God!
     It is he who is enthroned on high
     who looks upon heaven and earth below.
He raises the poor from the dust,
     lifts up the needy from the ashes,
to give them a place among the rulers,
     among the princes of his people.

To the barren woman he gives a household
and makes her the joyful mother of sons.

Glory be . . .

Antiphon

The Lord was with Joseph and guided him in all he did.

Reading

Mt 2:13–15, NRSV

After [the Wise Men] had left, an angel of the Lord appeared to Joseph in a dream and said, "Get up, take the child and his mother, and flee to Egypt, and remain there until I tell you; Herod is about to search for the child to destroy him." Then Joseph got up, took the child and his mother by night, and went to Egypt, and remained there until the death of Herod.

Reflection and spontaneous prayer of mind and heart.

Intercessions

Joseph, as you experienced the terror of fear and of flight, and the hardships of exile and homelessness, look with compassion upon all those who are fearful, exiled, and homeless.

Joseph, so prompt to obey the will of God, obtain for me the grace to accept God's will even if it means to endure suffering for the love of God.

Joseph, in all things God's servant, teach me to serve God with all my heart in whatever circumstances his loving will presents itself to me.

℣. Pray for us, Saint Joseph,

℟. That we may be made worthy of the promises of Christ.

Closing Prayer

O Lord, assisted by the prayers of the husband of your most holy Mother, grant that what we cannot obtain of ourselves, we may, through his intercession, be given by you who live and reign with the Father in the unity of the Holy Spirit, God for ever and ever. Amen.

May the divine assistance remain always with us.

And may the souls of the faithful departed through the mercy of God rest in peace. Amen.

Conclude with the Sign of the Cross.

Day Five

Invocation

O Lord, open my lips,
And my tongue will proclaim your praise.
Glory be to the Father, and to the Son, and to the
    Holy Spirit,
as it was in the beginning, is now, and will be
    forever. Amen.

Antiphon

The Lord has made me as a father to the king, the
master of his whole household.

Psalm 24

What must I do?

Who shall ascend the mountain of the LORD?
    Who will stand in his holy place?
The one of sinless hands and upright heart,
    whose soul does not yearn for what is vain,
    and does not swear deceitfully,

will draw blessings from the Lᴏʀᴅ
and justice from his saving God."

Glory be . . .

Antiphon

The Lord has made me as a father to the king, the master of his whole household.

Reading

Mt 2:19–23, NRSV

When Herod died, an angel of the Lord suddenly appeared in a dream to Joseph in Egypt and said, "Get up, take the child and his mother, and go to the land of Israel, for those who were seeking the child's life are dead." Then Joseph got up, took the child and his mother, and went to the land of Israel. But when he heard that Archelaus was ruling over Judea in place of his father Herod, he was afraid to go there. And after being warned in a dream, he went away to the district of Galilee. There he made his home in a town called Nazareth.

Reflection and spontaneous prayer of mind and heart.

Intercessions

Joseph, so tender and wise in providing for Jesus and Mary, teach me how to serve Christ in caring for those whom God has given me to love.

Joseph, by the fears you experienced for the life of the Child, teach me to fear the loss of the Christ-life in me, and to guard it carefully.

Joseph, head of the Holy Family of Nazareth, teach me how to take my place within my own family.

℣. Pray for us, Saint Joseph,

℟. That we may be made worthy of the promises of Christ.

Closing Prayer

O Lord, assisted by the prayers of the husband of your most holy Mother, grant that what we cannot obtain of ourselves, we may, through his intercession, be given by you who live and reign with the Father in the unity of the Holy Spirit, God for ever and ever. Amen.

May the divine assistance remain always with us.

And may the souls of the faithful departed through the mercy of God rest in peace. Amen.

Conclude with the Sign of the Cross.

Day Six

Invocation

O Lord, open my lips,
And my tongue will proclaim your praise.
Glory be to the Father, and to the Son, and to the
    Holy Spirit,
as it was in the beginning, is now, and will be
    forever. Amen.

Antiphon

Have no fear: I have been sent ahead of you to pre-serve your life.

Psalm 101, 131

Resolutions

I will the pursue the way of integrity,
When will it come to me!
I will conduct myself with an upright heart
among my own.
O Lord, my heart is not arrogant,
nor my eyes haughty;
nor do I run after greatness

or grand accomplishments beyond me.
I have stilled and calmed my spirit
as a weaned child resting on its mother;
like the weaned child, so is my spirit within me.

Glory be . . .

Antiphon

Have no fear: I have been sent ahead of you to preserve your life.

Reading

Lk 2:42–43, 46–49

And when he was twelve years old they went up to Jerusalem in accordance with the custom of the feast, and after they had fulfilled the days, while they were returning, the child Jesus remained in Jerusalem, but his parents did not know . . . And it happened that after three days they found him the Temple, seated in the midst of the teachers, both listening to them and asking him questions, and all those listening to him were amazed at his intelligence and his answers. When his parents saw him they were amazed and his mother said to him, "Son, why did you do this to us? You see your father and I have been looking for you, worried to death!" And he said to them, "Why were you looking for me? Did you not know that I have to concern myself with my Father's affairs?"

Reflection and spontaneous prayer of mind and heart.

Intercessions

Joseph, obtain for me the grace to always go in Mary's company in search of Jesus all the days of my life.

Joseph, pray to Jesus for me that after having looked for him all my life I may at last possess him in heaven for ever.

Joseph, teach me by your example to see the hand of God at work in the events and circumstances of my life.

℣. Pray for us, Saint Joseph,

℞. That we may be made worthy of the promises of Christ.

Closing Prayer

O Lord, assisted by the prayers of the husband of your most holy Mother, grant that what we cannot obtain of ourselves, we may, through his intercession, be given by you who live and reign with the Father in the unity of the Holy Spirit, God for ever and ever. Amen.

May the divine assistance remain always with us.

And may the souls of the faithful departed through the mercy of God rest in peace. Amen.

Conclude with the Sign of the Cross.

Day Seven

Invocation

O Lord, open my lips,

And my tongue will proclaim your praise.

Glory be to the Father, and to the Son, and to the Holy Spirit,

as it was in the beginning, is now, and will be forever. Amen.

Antiphon

The just man shall grow in grace, and flourish for ever in the sight of the Lord.

Psalm 3,4

Confidence

You, Lord, are a shield around me;
you are my glory and the One who holds my head
    high.
Since it is the Lord who upholds me,
As I lie down I fall asleep. When I rise
I have no fear of the myriads of people
stationed round about and against me.
The joy you have brought to my heart
is greater than that
which others receive from plentiful grain and wine.
In peace, let me fall asleep as soon as I lie down.
You alone, Lord, can make me rest securely.

Glory be . . .

Antiphon

The just man shall grow in grace, and flourish for
ever in the sight of the Lord.

Reading

Lk 2:22, 25, 27–35, NABRE

When the days were completed for their purifica-
tion according to the law of Moses, they took him up to

Jerusalem to present him to the Lord. . . . Now there was a man in Jerusalem whose name was Simeon. . . . It had been revealed to him by the holy Spirit that he should not see death before he had seen the Messiah of the Lord. He came in the Spirit into the temple; and . . . he took [the child Jesus] into his arms and blessed God, saying:

"Now, Master, you may let your servant go
     in peace, according to your word,
for my eyes have seen your salvation,
     which you prepared in sight of all the peoples,
a light for revelation to the Gentiles,
     and glory for your people Israel."

The child's father and mother were amazed at what was said about him, and Simeon blessed them and said to Mary his mother, "Behold this child is destined for the fall and rise of many in Israel, and to be a sign that will be contradicted (and you yourself a sword will pierce) so that the thoughts of many hearts may be revealed.

Reflection and spontaneous prayer of mind and heart.

Intercessions

Joseph, so faithful in obeying the law of God, teach me by your example to love and to live by the law of God.

Joseph, filled with wonder, obtain for me the grace to always be amazed when I think of the greatness of Jesus' love for me.

Joseph, hearing Simeon's prophecy, obtain for me the grace of tender compassion toward my Lord in his passion, and toward Mary in her sorrows.

℣. Pray for us, Saint Joseph,

℟. That we may be made worthy of the promises of Christ.

Closing Prayer

O Lord, assisted by the prayers of the husband of your most holy Mother, grant that what we cannot obtain of ourselves, we may, through his intercession, be given by you who live and reign with the Father in the unity of the Holy Spirit, God for ever and ever. Amen.

May the divine assistance remain always with us.

And may the souls of the faithful departed through the mercy of God rest in peace. Amen.

Conclude with the Sign of the Cross.

Day Eight

Invocation

O Lord, open my lips,

And my tongue will proclaim your praise.

Glory be to the Father, and to the Son, and to the
Holy Spirit,

as it was in the beginning, is now, and will be
forever. Amen.

Antiphon

Jesus went down to Nazareth with them and lived in obedience to them.

Psalm 27

Unshaken Trust

The LORD is my light and my salvation,
who can I fear?

The Lord is my life's stronghold,
of whom can I be afraid?
When evil doers drew near to me
to devour my flesh,
when my adversaries and enemies were against me,
it was they who stumbled and fell.
Should an army encamp against me,
my heart would not fear;
should war rage against me,
even then would I trust.
One thing have I asked of the Lord, this I seek:
to dwell in the house of the Lord
all the days of my life,
gazing on the goodness of the Lord
and seeking guidance in his Temple.
For he will conceal me in his tent on an evil day
and hide me in the shelter of his dwelling;
he will set me in the shelter of his tent.

Glory be . . .

Antiphon

Jesus went down to Nazareth with them and lived
in obedience to them.

Reading

Lk 2:51–52

Then [Jesus] went down with them and went to Nazareth, and he was subject to them. His mother kept all these things in her heart, and Jesus progressed in wisdom and age and grace before God and men.

Reflection and spontaneous prayer of mind and heart.

Intercessions

Joseph, teacher of the Son of God, teach me how to work with and for our Lord in everything I do.

Joseph, glory of family life, through your intercession obtain for all families the happiness found in harmony and unity.

Joseph, happy to die in the arms of Jesus and Mary, bring comfort and peace to all those enduring the last moments of their life on earth.

℣. Pray for us, Saint Joseph,

℟. That we may be made worthy of the promises of Christ.

Closing Prayer

O Lord, assisted by the prayers of the husband of your most holy Mother, grant that what we cannot obtain of ourselves, we may, through his intercession, be given by you who live and reign with the Father in the unity of the Holy Spirit, God for ever and ever. Amen.

May the divine assistance remain always with us.

And may the souls of the faithful departed through the mercy of God rest in peace. Amen.

Conclude with the Sign of the Cross.

DAY NINE

Invocation

O Lord, open my lips,

And my tongue will proclaim your praise.

Glory be to the Father, and to the Son, and to the
    Holy Spirit,

as it was in the beginning, is now, and will be
    forever. Amen.

Antiphon

When the people came to him in their need, he told them, "Go to Joseph."

Psalm 84

Desire for God

Lord God of hosts,
>   hear my prayer,
>   listen, O God of Jacob.
Behold, O God, our shield,
>   and look on the face of your anointed.
One day in your courts is better than a thousand
>   elsewhere.
I would rather stand at the threshold of God's
>   house
>   than live in the dwelling of the wicked.
Truly, the Lord is sun and shield;
>   the Lord grants favor and splendor;
>   he will not withhold any good from those who
>   live an upright life.
Lord of hosts,
>   happy the one who trusts in you.
Glory be . . .

Antiphon

When the people came to him in their need, he told them, "Go to Joseph."

Reading

After this I looked, and behold a vast crowd which no one could ever count from every nation, tribe, people, and tongue, standing before the throne and the Lamb and dressed in long white robes with palm branches in their hands. There were crying out in a loud voice and saying,

"Victory to our God Who is seated
upon the throne,
and to the Lamb!"

Then all the angels stood around the throne, the elders, and the living creatures. They fell on their faces before the throne and worshipped God saying,

"Amen! Blessing, glory, wisdom, thanks, honor,
power, and might
be to our God forever and ever, amen!"

Reflection and spontaneous prayer of mind and heart.

Intercessions

Joseph, greatest among the humble whom God has exalted, receive the praise we offer you.

Joseph, intercessor before God on behalf of the whole Church, hear our prayers.

Joseph, united for ever to Jesus and Mary, welcome me and all men and women into your company in heaven.

℣. Pray for us, Saint Joseph,

℟. That we may be made worthy of the promises of Christ.

Closing Prayer

O Lord, assisted by the prayers of the husband of your most holy Mother, grant that what we cannot obtain of ourselves, we may, through his intercession, be given by you who live and reign with the Father in the unity of the Holy Spirit, God for ever and ever. Amen.

May the divine assistance remain always with us.

And may the souls of the faithful departed through the mercy of God rest in peace. Amen.

Conclude with the Sign of the Cross.

Holy Cloak of Saint Joseph

Throughout history a cloak has been the symbol of belonging. When we seek to take refuge under the cloak of Saint Joseph, we are asking to become a member of his family, along with Jesus and Mary. In the following prayers, prayed each day for thirty days, we ask Saint Joseph to enfold us in his cloak: to protect us, to guide us, and to shelter us from evil.

In the name of the Father, and of the Son, and of the Holy Spirit. Amen.

Jesus, Mary, and Joseph, I give you my heart and my soul.

Recite the Glory Be three times in thanksgiving to the Holy Trinity for having exalted Saint Joseph to a position of such exceptional dignity.

Offering

O great patriarch, Saint Joseph, I bow before you and ask you to accept me within the folds of your holy cloak. I promise to honor you throughout my life and to prove my love for you.

Help me, Saint Joseph. Assist me now and throughout my life, but especially at the moment of my death, as you were assisted by Jesus and Mary, so that I may honor you forever in heaven. Amen.

O glorious patriarch, Saint Joseph, I bow before you and offer you homage and true devotion, remembering the numerous virtues which adorn your holy person. In you was fulfilled the mysterious dream of Joseph, the son of Jacob (see Gen 37:9). Not only did the divine sun, Jesus, surround you with the shining splendor of his rays, but the mystic moon, the Virgin Mary, shone upon you with her soft, reflected light. At your request, will not Jesus and Mary, who honor you and give you their appreciation and trust, help me also to honor you in this novena?

O great saint, ask that the Lord may look upon me with benevolence. And, just as Joseph in ancient times did not reject his guilty brothers (see Gen 42–50) but accepted them with love, protected them, and saved them from hunger and death, so you, O glorious patriarch, through your intercession, ask that the Lord may never abandon me in this valley of exile. Please ask also that I may have the grace to always be numbered among your devoted servants who live serenely under the cloak of your protection, every day of my life and at the moment when I breathe my last breath. Amen.

Prayers

Hail, O glorious Saint Joseph, you who are entrusted with the priceless treasures of heaven and who are the foster father of the One who nourishes all the creatures of the universe. You are, after the most Blessed Virgin Mary, the saint most worthy of love and devotion. You had the honor of raising, guiding, nourishing, and embracing the Messiah, whom so many kings and prophets desired to behold.

Saint Joseph, obtain for me, through the divine mercy of God, the grace for which I humbly beg as well as graces for the holy souls in purgatory.

Recite the Glory Be three times.

O powerful Saint Joseph, Patron of the Universal Church, I invoke you, above all the other saints, as the greatest protector of the afflicted, and I offer gratitude to your heart, which is always ready to help anyone in need.

O beloved Saint Joseph, widows, orphans, abandoned, afflicted, and wretched of every kind come to you with trust and confidence. There is no sorrow, anguish, or misfortune which you have not consoled. I beg you to use, on my behalf, the gifts God has given you, so that I, too, may be granted an answer to my petition. And you, holy souls in purgatory, pray to Saint Joseph for me.

Recite the Glory Be three times.

O Saint Joseph, you have interceded for so many others before me who invoked you for comfort, peace, grace, and favor. My sad and sorrowful soul cannot find peace amid the trials that beset me. O beloved saint, in God you know all my needs even before I say them in prayer. You know how much I need God's grace. I bow before you, and I sigh, O beloved Saint Joseph, from beneath the heavy burden that oppresses me. There is no human heart to whom I can confide my troubles. Even if I were to receive pity from some charitable soul, I could not be helped. I turn to you, hoping that you will not reject me and remembering that Saint Teresa of Ávila said that she did not recall ever having asked you for anything that you failed to grant.

O Saint Joseph, comforter of the afflicted, take pity on me in my sorrow and lead the holy souls in purgatory, who invest so much hope in our prayers, into God's light and happiness.

Recite the Glory Be three times.

O sublime Saint, by your most perfect obedience
    to God, take pity on me.
By your holy life, full of grace and merit, hear my
    prayer.
By your most sweet name, claim me.
By your most generous heart, assist me.
By your most holy tears, comfort me.
By your seven sorrows, sustain me.
By your seven joys, console my heart.
From all harm to body and soul, protect me.
From all danger and disaster, save me.

Assist me and the dear souls in purgatory by your powerful intercession. I ask that you obtain for me all that I need, particularly the grace for which I ask today.

Recite the Glory Be three times.

O glorious Saint Joseph, countless are the graces and favors you have obtained for afflicted souls. Sick people and those who are oppressed, persecuted, betrayed, bereft of all human comfort, and in need of bread and support implore your royal protection and are granted their petitions. Do not permit, O dearest Saint Joseph, that I alone among all others who have appealed to you should be denied this petition that I now beg of you. Show yourself powerful and generous, even to me, and I will thank you and bless you forever, Holy Patriarch, Saint Joseph, my great protector and, in particular, the intercessor of the holy souls in purgatory.

Recite the Glory Be three times.

O eternal God, through the merits of Jesus and Mary, I beg you to grant my petition. In the name of Jesus and Mary I prostrate myself before your divine Presence, and I beg you to accept my firm decision to persevere among those who live under the patronage of Saint Joseph. Extend your blessing on this precious treasury of prayers that I dedicate to Saint Joseph today as a pledge of my devotion.

Recite the Glory Be three times.

Supplications in Honor of Saint Joseph's Hidden Life with Jesus and Mary

Saint Joseph, beg Jesus to come into my soul
and sanctify it.

Saint Joseph, beg Jesus to come into my heart
and inspire it with charity.

Saint Joseph, beg Jesus to come into my mind
and enlighten it.

Saint Joseph, beg Jesus to come into my will
and strengthen it.

Saint Joseph, beg Jesus to come into my thoughts
and purify them.

Saint Joseph, beg Jesus to come into my affections
and regulate them.

Saint Joseph, beg Jesus to come into my desires
and direct them.

Saint Joseph, beg Jesus to come into my deeds
and bless them.

Saint Joseph, obtain for me Jesus' holy love.

Saint Joseph, obtain for me from Jesus the grace
to imitate your virtues.

Saint Joseph, obtain for me from Jesus true
humility of spirit.

Saint Joseph, obtain for me from Jesus peace in my soul.

Saint Joseph, obtain for me from Jesus a holy fear of the Lord.

Saint Joseph, obtain for me from Jesus a strong desire for sanctity.

Saint Joseph, obtain for me from Jesus a gentle character.

Saint Joseph, obtain for me from Jesus a pure and charitable heart.

Saint Joseph, obtain for me from Jesus the grace to bear life's sufferings with patience.

Saint Joseph, obtain for me from Jesus wisdom of faith.

Saint Joseph, obtain for me from Jesus perseverance in doing good.

Saint Joseph, obtain for me from Jesus the strength to carry my crosses.

Saint Joseph, obtain for me from Jesus detachment from earthly goods.

Saint Joseph, obtain for me from Jesus the grace always to walk the narrow path toward heaven.

Saint Joseph, obtain for me from Jesus the grace to avoid all occasions of sin.

Saint Joseph, obtain for me from Jesus a holy desire for heaven.

Saint Joseph, obtain for me from Jesus the grace of final perseverance.

Saint Joseph, do not abandon me.

Saint Joseph, grant that my heart may never cease to love you and that my lips may always praise you.

Saint Joseph, as you so loved Jesus, help me to love him also.

Saint Joseph, graciously accept me as your devoted servant.

Saint Joseph, I entrust myself to you; accept me and help me.

Saint Joseph, do not abandon me at the hour of my death.

Jesus, Mary, and Joseph, I give you my heart and my soul.

Invocations to Saint Joseph

Remember, O most chaste spouse of the Blessed Virgin Mary, my beloved protector, that no one who called upon you for protection and asked you for help was ever known to be denied comfort. Thus, I confidently turn to you and fervently commend myself to you.

O Saint Joseph, listen to my prayer, accept it with compassion, and help me. Amen.

Glorious Saint Joseph, spouse of Mary and earthly father of Jesus, think of me, watch over me. Teach me to work for my sanctification and take merciful heed of the urgent needs which I entrust to your fatherly care.

Protect me from obstacles and difficulties so that what I ask for may always be only for the greater glory of God and for the benefit of my soul.

As a pledge of my deep gratitude, I promise to spread the word of your glories, while offering heartfelt blessings to the Lord, who granted you so much power in heaven and upon earth.

Litany of Saint Joseph, p. 184.

Closing Prayer

O glorious patriarch, Saint Joseph, who were chosen by God to be the head and guardian of the most holy of families, stoop down from heaven to be the guardian of my soul and envelop me in the cloak of your protection. From this moment on, I choose you as a father, a protector, and a guide. I place my soul, my body, all that I possess, all that I am, my life, and my death under your special care. Look upon me as your son/daughter; defend me against all my enemies, visible and invisible. Assist me in my need; console me in all of life's bitterness, and especially when I am upon my deathbed. Pray for me to our precious Redeemer who as a child was held in your arms and those of your dearly beloved spouse, the glorious Virgin Mary. I beg you to ask God for the graces I need for my real good, for my everlasting salvation. I will strive to be worthy of your special patronage. Amen.

Practices

A Holy Hour with Saint Joseph

A Holy Hour, the tradition of spending an hour in Eucharistic adoration in the presence of the Blessed Sacrament, places Jesus at the center of our prayer. It is also customary to pray "in the company" of the Blessed Mother or one of the saints. Those devoted to Saint Joseph can focus their reflections on him and invite him into this time of deeper prayer, allowing him to be their guide.

The outline for this Holy Hour follows a method inspired by the Pauline spirituality of Blessed James Alberione, founder of the Pauline Family. The Holy Hour has three parts or "moments," based on Jesus' definition of himself as Way, Truth, and Life (Jn 14:6). In the first part we read and ponder a Scripture passage, listening attentively to the truth God wants to speak to us. In the second part we take a closer look at our own lives and make an examination of conscience. In the third part we place our needs, those of the Church, and those of the world before our loving God, praying spontaneously, or praying the Rosary or other favorite prayers.

FIRST MOMENT

Ask for the light of the Holy Spirit and ask Saint Joseph to guide you through the contemplation of the Scripture passages. You can choose one or more of the following selections.

Luke 2:21–35 Presentation of Jesus to the Temple

Matthew 2:13–23 The Flight into Egypt

Luke 2:39–51 Finding Jesus in the Temple

At the conclusion of your reflections, pray the prayer In Praise of Saint Joseph, p. 43.

SECOND MOMENT

Recall those times you experienced the loving action of God in your life, and then pray an act of thanksgiving for these graces and blessings. Now take a few moments to examine your thoughts, actions, attitudes, and motivations; speak to the Lord about what is in your heart that is sinful. How do you need to change in order to be more Christ-like? Pray an act of sorrow and allow the healing work of grace to penetrate your soul.

After praying an act of sorrow, pray the prayer to Saint Joseph To Lead a Virtuous Life, p. 107.

THIRD MOMENT

Speak to Jesus about your deepest desires for yourself and for your loved ones. Ask for the graces you and your loved ones need to lead lives of integrity and holiness; then you may pray one of the following:

The Rosary in Honor of Saint Joseph, p. 176.

The Litany of Saint Joseph, p. 184.

To You, O Blessed Joseph, p. 145.

Meditative Reading

IN THE PRACTICE of meditative reading, we use the power of our reason and understanding to reflect on what we read. As we ponder the words and think about their meaning, we are opening our mind to what the Holy Spirit wants to say to us concerning the direction of our life.

— Choose a suitable time and a relaxed atmosphere.

— Pray for the light of the Holy Spirit and select the passage for your meditation. (See below for some possibilities.)

— Read the passage slowly, two or three times.

— Ponder the passage and ask: In what way(s) is the passage speaking to me, personally? What is God saying to me? What is God asking of me today? How will I respond to God's invitation today? Are there changes I need to make in my attitude or my behavior?

— Make your resolution, then offer a prayer in honor of Saint Joseph, asking for his guidance.

Joseph is a "protector" because he is able to hear God's voice and be guided by his will; and for this reason he is all the more sensitive to the persons entrusted to his safekeeping. He can look at things realistically, he is in touch with his surroundings, he can make truly wise decisions. In him, dear friends, we learn how to respond to God's call, readily and willingly, but we also see the core of the Christian vocation, which is Christ! Let us protect Christ in our lives, so that we can protect others, so that we can protect creation.

Pope Francis (Homily, March 19, 2013)

From the example of Saint Joseph we all receive a strong invitation to carry out with fidelity, simplicity, and modesty the task that Providence has entrusted to us. I think especially of fathers and mothers of families, and I pray that they will always be able to appreciate the beauty of a simple and industrious life, cultivating the conjugal relationship with care and fulfilling with enthusiasm the great and difficult educational mission.

To priests, who exercise a paternal role over ecclesial communities, may Saint Joseph help them love the Church with affection and complete dedication, and may he support consecrated persons in their joyous and faithful observance of the evangelical counsels of poverty, chastity, and obedience. May he protect workers throughout the world so that they contribute with their different professions to the progress of the whole of humanity, and may he help every Christian to fulfill God's will with confidence and love, thereby cooperating in the fulfillment of the work of salvation.

Pope Emeritus Benedict XVI
(Angelus Message March 19, 2006)

What is crucially important here is the sanctification of daily life, a sanctification which each person must acquire according to his or her own state, and one which can be promoted to a model accessible to all people. Saint Joseph is the model of those humble ones that Christianity raises up to great destinies; . . . he is proof that in order to be a good and genuine follower of Christ, there is no need of great things—it is enough to have the common, simple and human virtues, but they need to be true and authentic.

Saint John Paul II (Redemptoris Custos, 24)

We picture Joseph, the lover of silence, as being totally dedicated to his humble and hardworking life, choosing obscurity, disinclined to public attention or to socialize with the townsfolk without a serious reason for doing so. But he was not a recluse. His work brought him in frequent contact with people. He knew how to be cordial and deal with strangers. But at the same time he was polite, discreet, reserved, one who wasted neither words nor time. He would return quickly to the intimacy of his family. Silence and recollection greatly fostered his peace of heart, his joy in intimate union with God, his prayer life, and his growth in grace. Thus, his life became very precious in the eyes of God.

Reverand G. Pasquali, SSP (Pauline Spirituality)

In Saint Joseph, God truly found a faithful servant whose eyes were ever toward him to learn God's desires and his will, to carry them out promptly, docilely, and lovingly.

Yes, sanctity consists in conformity to the will of God, union with God. It consists not in exterior acts but in interior ones—that is, in thinking and willing what God wants. External works follow as a consequence.

There should be interior docility—the willingness to say "yes" to God always. Not just "yes" in what is required by the Commandments, but also "yes" to the daily responsibilities stemming from one's chosen calling in life. The wisdom of God guides man rightly: "The Lord leads the just man along the right path." This is the wisdom which surpasses all other wisdom.

Blessed James Alberione (Sermon March 19, 1959)

Prayerful persons, in particular, should love [Saint Joseph] as a father. I do not know how anyone can think of the Queen of Angels, at the time when she was undergoing so much with the Child Jesus, without giving thanks to Saint Joseph for looking after them in the way he did. If anyone has not a guide to teach him how to pray, let him take this glorious saint as his master and he will not go astray.

All I ask, for the love of God, is that anyone who does not believe me will put what I say to the test, and they will then learn for themselves how advantageous it is to commend oneself to this glorious patriarch Joseph and to have a special devotion to him.

Saint Teresa of Ávila (Autobiography, ch. 6, 42–43)

The Cord of Saint Joseph

IN THE EARLY Church the wearing of a cord or cincture was a symbol of chastity as well as mortification and humility. The wearing of a cord in honor of a saint is also an ancient practice.

The practice of wearing the cord of Saint Joseph has its origin in the small town of Antwerp, Belgium. An Augustinian nun, Sister Elizabeth, was suffering from a painful illness, which doctors said would lead to her death. Having a special devotion to Saint Joseph, she asked that a cincture be blessed in his honor; then she wrapped the cord around her waist. A few days later, praying through the intercession of Saint Joseph, Sister Elizabeth realized that she was completely pain-free. After examining her, the doctors concluded that the cure was miraculous.

The cord of Saint Joseph, a white, braided cotton cable, is worn around the waist and has seven knots, which symbolize the seven sorrows and seven joys of Saint Joseph. The cincture is worn primarily as a support in living the virtues of chastity and purity of heart, as well as for special protection, assistance at the hour of death, and at times for relief from physical ailments.

Saint Joseph Oil

FOLLOWING A PRACTICE that was in use in France, Saint Andre Bessette (1845–1937) distributed Saint Joseph Oil to the sick and instructed them to rub it on the affected area of their body and pray to Saint Joseph for relief from their pain. Continuing this tradition, at Saint Joseph's Oratory in Montreal, Quebec, there is a basin of oil in front of a statue of Saint Joseph. Floating in the oil is a wick that burns as a perpetual votive lamp. The oil is then bottled and is available through the online store of the Oratory.

Saint Joseph Table

THE TRADITION OF the Saint Joseph Table or the Saint Joseph Altar dates as far back as the Middle Ages, when a severe drought devastated the island of Sicily and many were dying of famine.

The people prayed for rain through the intercession of Saint Joseph, promising that if God allowed it to rain, the citizens would prepare a feast in honor of their patron and invite everyone in the area, especially the less fortunate. The rains came, the crops flourished, and with the food from their harvest the people prepared *La Tavola di San Giuseppe* to show their gratitude.

Through the centuries the tradition of the Saint Joseph Table has been not only a symbolic thank you for a favor received, but also a renewal of devotion to Saint Joseph. The custom still exists in several American cities where there are significant Sicilian populations or people of Italian ancestry. The Table itself can take many forms according to the tradition of the town, village, or city of origin. It can be as simple as a single table, or as intricate as several tables and tiers. The shape of a more elaborate altar is generally oblong, set vertically with extensions on either side to resemble a cross, and with three levels representing the Holy Trinity. In the center of the top level is placed a sizeable statue of Saint Joseph holding the Christ Child. The tables are draped in white and decorated with flowers, fruits, meatless foods, breads, and sweets. These are meant to feed not only friends and relatives but also, traditionally, hungry strangers and anyone who visits the Table.

Family Prayer—
Blessing for a Saint Joseph Table

We honor you, Saint Joseph, on this your feast day,
as we gather with family and friends
to celebrate our gratitude for the many favors
you have bestowed on us.
Guardian of the Holy Family,
we call on you today to be
our patron, father, and protector,
and ask that you watch over us,
our families, and our loved ones.
Just as the food we have prepared
will nourish our bodies,
may we always seek to nourish one another's spirits
with love, compassion, kindness, and gratitude.
Through your intercession, dear Saint Joseph,
we ask that the blessing of God,
Father, Son, and Holy Spirit
come down upon us
and remain with us forever. Amen.

Saint Joseph Bread

Saint Joseph Bread is served on Saint Joseph's feast day, March 19, and is traditionally prepared for the Saint Joseph Altar. The bread usually has the texture of a homestyle white bread with a somewhat sweet taste, sometimes flavored with anise, and/or containing golden raisins. The dough can be shaped into various designs for loaves that will decorate the Saint Joseph Table. Common forms related to Saint Joseph could be a crown, a cross, a staff, a wreath, carpenter tools, etc.

Fava Beans

Fava beans are customarily served in some form on the feast of Saint Joseph. A popular dish for a Saint Joseph Table is a fava bean-based minestra (soup) served with Saint Joseph Bread.

The tradition of the fava bean began during a famine in Sicily, where the bean had been used as fodder for cattle. Although most of the crops failed, the fava bean thrived in the poor, rocky soil. In order to survive, the farmers prepared them in various ways for their family meals and were grateful to have them; hence their connection to Saint Joseph, who is invoked as a model of trust in Divine Providence.

Further Reading

Calloway, Donald H., Rev. *Consecration to Saint Joseph*. Stockbridge: Marian Press, 2020.

Hermes, Kathryn James. *St. Joseph: Help for Life's Emergencies*. Boston: Pauline Books & Media, 2009.

John Paul II. *Guardian of the Redeemer*. 1989. Anniversary edition with commentary by Dr. Joseph C. Atkinson. Boston: Pauline Books & Media, 2014.

Pope Francis. *Patris Corde*. Apostolic letter, December 8, 2020. http://www.vatican.va/content/francesco/en/apost_letters/documents/papa-francesco-lettera-ap_20201208_patris-corde.html.

List of Contributors

Pauline
BOOKS & MEDIA

A mission of the Daughters of St. Paul

As apostles of Jesus Christ,
evangelizing today's world:

We are CALLED to holiness
by God's living Word and Eucharist.

We COMMUNICATE the Gospel message
through our lives and through all
available forms of media.

We SERVE the Church
by responding to the hopes and needs
of all people with the Word of God,
in the spirit of St. Paul.

For more information visit us at www.pauline.org.

Pauline
BOOKS & MEDIA

The Daughters of St. Paul operate book and media centers at the following addresses. Visit, call or write the one nearest you today, or find us at www.paulinestore.org.

CALIFORNIA
3908 Sepulveda Blvd, Culver City, CA 90230   310-397-8676
3250 Middlefield Road, Menlo Park, CA 94025   650-562-7060

FLORIDA
145 S.W. 107th Avenue, Miami, FL 33174   305-559-6715

HAWAII
1143 Bishop Street, Honolulu, HI 96813   808-521-2731

ILLINOIS
172 North Michigan Avenue, Chicago, IL 60601   312-346-4228

LOUISIANA
4403 Veterans Memorial Blvd, Metairie, LA 70006   504-887-7631

MASSACHUSETTS
885 Providence Hwy, Dedham, MA 02026   781-326-5385

MISSOURI
9804 Watson Road, St. Louis, MO 63126   314-965-3512

NEW YORK
115 E. 29th Street, New York City, NY 10016   212-754-1110

SOUTH CAROLINA
243 King Street, Charleston, SC 29401   843-577-0175

VIRGINIA
1025 King Street, Alexandria, VA 22314   703-549-3806

CANADA
3022 Dufferin Street, Toronto, ON M6B 3T5   416-781-9131